For Jeanne Kildde
with my best wishes.

William Westfall

This book has been published in conjunction with the
150th anniversary of the founding of the University
of Trinity College.

McGILL-QUEEN'S STUDIES IN THE HISTORY OF RELIGION

Volumes in this series have been supported by the Jackman Foundation of Toronto.

SERIES TWO In memory of George Rawlyk
Donald Harman Akenson, Editor

A Social History of the Cloister
Daily Life in the Teaching
Monasteries of the Old Regime
Elizabeth Rapley

Households of Faith
Family, Gender, and Community in
Canada, 1760–1969
Nancy Christie, editor

Blood Ground
Colonialism, Missions, and the
Contest for Christianity in the
Cape Colony and Britain,
1799–1853
Elizabeth Elbourne

A History of Canadian Catholics
Gallicanism, Romanism, and
Canadianism
Terence J. Fay

Archbishop Stagni's Reports on the
Ontario Bilingual Schools
Question, 1915
*Translated and Edited by John
Zucchi*

The Founding Moment
Church, Society, and the
Construction of Trinity College
William Westfall

The Cross and the Star of David
The Holocaust, Israel, and
Canadian Protestant Churches
Haim Genizi

SERIES TWO
G.A. Rawlyk, Editor

1 Small Differences
Irish Catholics and Irish
Protestants, 1815–1922
An International Perspective
Donald Harman Akenson

2 Two Worlds
The Protestant Culture of Nine-
teenth-Century Ontario
William Westfall

3 An Evangelical Mind
Nathanael Burwash and the
Methodist Tradition in Canada,
1839–1918
Marguerite Van Die

4 The Dévotes
Women and Church in
Seventeenth-Century France
Elizabeth Rapley

5 The Evangelical Century
College and Creed in English
Canada from the Great Revival
to the Great Depression
Michael Gauvreau

6 The German Peasants' War
and Anabaptist Community
of Goods
James M. Stayer

7 A World Mission
Canadian Protestantism and the
Quest for a New International
Order, 1918–1939
Robert Wright

8 Serving the Present Age
Revivalism, Progressivism,
and the Methodist Tradition
in Canada
Phyllis D. Airhart

THE FOUNDING MOMENT

*Church, Society, and the
Construction of Trinity College*

William Westfall

McGill-Queen's University Press
Montreal & Kingston • London • Ithaca

© McGill-Queen's University Press, 2002
ISBN 0-7735-2447-9

Legal deposit second quarter 2002
Bibliothèque nationale du Québec

Printed in Canada on acid-free paper that is 100% ancient forest free (100% post-consumer recycled), processed chlorine free, and printed with vegetable-based, low VOC inks.

McGill-Queen's University Press acknowledges the support of the Canada Council for the Arts for its publishing program. It also acknowledges the financial support of the Government of Canada through the Book Publishing Industry Development Program (BPIDP).

National Library of Canada Cataloguing in Publication Data

Westfall, William, 1945–
   The founding moment : church, society, and the construction of Trinity College

(McGill-Queen's studies in the history of religion)
Includes bibliographical references and index.
ISBN 0-7735-2447-9

   1. Trinity College (Toronto, Ont.) – History. I. Title. II. Series

LE3.T72W47 2002   378.713541   C2002-900614-7

This book was designed by David LeBlanc and typeset in 10.2/14 Sabon

Contents

Preface and Acknowledgments

This book, which grew out of the Larkin-Stuart lectures I delivered in November 2001, celebrates the sesquicentenary of Trinity College. Its title refers to one of the most remarkable aspects of the college's history: the founder, Bishop Strachan, argued that there was a precise moment when the college began. Unlike King's College, whose beginnings were mired in postponements and delays, Trinity was created with enormous energy and haste in response to a single event that the bishop believed threatened to alter the proper course of history irrevocably. The book begins, then, where the founder began, and it asks a simple question: What created this founding moment?

In trying to answer this question, I soon discovered that it was necessary to analyse critically the answer that the founder himself had given to the same question. Strachan placed the founding of Trinity in what historians might now call a discourse of secularization, for as the state removed the church from King's College, the Anglican Church felt compelled to found a new university that would restore the essential bond between religion and higher education. While this account of the founding acknowledges in part the important changes that were taking place in the relationship between religion and Canadian society, it also obscures other important issues that played an important part in the founding of Trinity College. The study tries to step behind the founding story and ask a second set of questions: What was the character of this new church college? What were its founding doctrines, and how were they translated into a real college with a curriculum, a faculty, a set of rules and regulations, and a collegiate culture? To answer these questions the study draws on a wide range of sources, including official college documents, student reminiscences, financial records, biographical files, architectural drawings, town plans, and personal correspondence. At the same time I have tried to consider issues of culture, social class, and gender that have not figured prominently in the official histories of such institutions.

The third series of questions approach the founding of the college from a different direction. Trinity was born in controversy, for many individuals and groups, both inside and outside the college, did not accept the social, religious, and cultural world that Strachan and the other founders were trying to create. They also resisted the course the bishop and the provost were determined to pursue, either challenging the college or supporting other educational institutions. In effect, the history of Trinity did not follow the progressive, triumphal path that supporters of the college had foretold (and that official historians are accustomed to follow). Why these groups opposed Trinity College, and what their opposition meant to the ability of the college to sustain its founding vision are important questions that this study tries to answer.

In effect this book "deconstructs" the construction of Trinity

College in order to tell the story of how an important group of Anglicans, both clerical and lay, responded to the social forces that were reshaping English Canada in the middle of the nineteenth century. In the enclosed, exclusively Anglican, and highly regulated world of Trinity College they hoped to find an asylum that was set apart from the new secular state and in which they could nurture the social and religious values they esteemed and prepare young men for both the church and the world. But within thirty years the opposition engendered by their programme had led to a host of problems that threatened the college's very existence. In time, these problems forced the college to reconsider many of its founding doctrines, build itself on a new foundation, and assume a very different relationship with the modern world.

A few words should be said about terminology. Anyone who has ventured into the religious history of the mid-nineteenth century is aware of the confusion caused by frequent changes in names. As a rule this study seeks clarity even at the price of strict accuracy. The names Upper Canada, Canada West, and Ontario all represent more or less the same civil jurisdiction, and people at the time continued to use older terms long after they had been replaced officially. When this study begins, the Diocese of Toronto, which was yet to be divided into the Diocese of Huron (in 1857) and the Diocese of Ontario (in 1862), included all of what is now Ontario, as far north as the Hudson Bay watershed. Trinity College was tied to the United Church of England and Ireland, and I use this name when it is clear from the context that the official name is required. Otherwise I use church or Anglican Church – the word Anglican was gaining popularity in the Victorian period. The people who were members of the church are a little more difficult to name. Here the study again uses the term Anglican to replace the cumbersome "members of the United Church of England and Ireland" or the now problematic "churchmen." The study also expands the collective noun "clergy" to include individual clergymen; this usage, of course, does not alter the fact all the clergy at this time were men.

I would like to thank first of all the members of the Larkin-Stuart committee (representatives of Trinity College and the Church of St Thomas) who honoured me with the invitation to present these endowed lectures, and to thank as well the audience, which responded so warmly to the presentations. The provost, Thomas Delworth, supported strongly the transformation of the lectures into this book, and Philip Arthur, chair of the Board of Trustees, undertook to raise funds to help defray the cost of the special sesquicentennial edition; his appeal was answered by many members of my year. Linda Corman, college librarian, placed the resources of the Graham Library at my disposal, and Henri Pilon, college archivist, allowed me access to valuable documentary sources and permitted me to reproduce some of them to illustrate the volume. Archivists and librarians at the City of Toronto Archives, the Toronto Reference Library, the Ontario Archives, the General Synod Archives, the Diocese of Toronto Archives, and the University of Toronto Archives have been enormously helpful; I offer special thanks to Maureen Morin of the Digital Studio, University of Toronto, for her help in transferring archival photographs, and John Dawson, the York University photographer, who oversaw the complicated process of image reproduction. Stephen Otto's awesome knowledge of matters urban and architectural helped me greatly on several occasions. The publication of the book was enthusiastically supported by Donald Akenson, editor of McGill-Queen's University Press, who is everything one could hope for in an editor. Joan McGilvray oversaw the preparation of the manuscript for publication, while the fine editing by

Freya Godard provided salutary discipline to the natural enthusiasms of my prose style. In writing this study I have relied heavily upon research I have undertaken as part of an ongoing study (co-directed by Professor Thomas McIntire) on the social and theological formation of Anglican clergy in the Diocese of Toronto. Financial support for this project has been generously provided by Trinity College, the Anglican Foundation, York University, and especially the Lilly Endowment.

I have tried to acknowledge in the endnotes the many scholars whose work serves as the building blocks of this study. I owe a special debt, however, to four people. Elizabeth Smyth read the manuscript and offered me the benefit of her deep understanding of the relationship between faith, institutionalized religion, and education. Wyn Millar and Bob Gidney, who kindly oversaw my belated entry into the history of schooling, also read the manuscript and successfully blocked my headlong rush over many an interpretive precipice. Cathy James sustained my spirits throughout this endeavour and guided me carefully through matters relating to gender and sexuality. Their criticisms, friendship, and encouragement were among the most memorable pleasures of writing this history.

THE FOUNDING MOMENT

I

The Grand Procession

On Wednesday 30 April 1851, an elaborate procession assembled in front of the Church of St George the Martyr, West Toronto. Led by the gentlemen beadles, it moved south along John Street to Queen, where it turned to the west and continued for about a mile to an open field beside an "elmy dale." Here this grand cavalcade of Anglicans was to celebrate the laying of the cornerstone of Trinity College. The whole spectacle, we are told, was "gay and animating in the extreme."[1] Near the head of the procession were the pupils of St Paul's Church Grammar School, accompanied by their masters. Two of the boys carried a cream-coloured banner with gold and rose lettering. They were followed by the contractors and clerk of the works, the members of the faculties of the new college, a large convocation of clergy, the college board, the architect, and various college officials. Behind them were the students in medicine and the students in divinity, the professors, and the college council. At the end of the procession, in the position of honour and authority, came the founder of Trinity College, the Rt Revd John Strachan, Lord Bishop of Toronto. He was preceded immediately by his chaplain and flanked by the two archdeacons of the diocese. The procession was escorted along the whole of the route by contributors and friends of the new college, some on foot, others in carriages.

On the college grounds had been erected a large platform, which was now crowded with ladies "anxious to witness ... the solemn and impressive" ceremony that was about to begin. When Bishop Strachan rose to address this multitude, which numbered some "several thousand persons," he was determined to explain the significance of the events that had brought such an impressive array to this site. He began with the recent demise of King's College, the university he had laboured for so many years to build up and defend. Indeed, Strachan bound together the destruction of King's and the founding of Trinity by recalling to his audience the twenty-third day of April, 1842, when "some of us assisted at the laying [of] the foundation stone of the University of King's College, with promising hopes and sincere prayers." But "vain and fleeting are the works and hopes of men." On the first day of January 1850, Robert Baldwin's University Act had severed the essential bond between religion and education, destroying the "noble seminary" of King's College and creating in its stead that godless abomination, the University of Toronto. So we are gathered on this spring day, the bishop declared, to restore what has been lost – to "seek with increasing faith the divine aid in this our second and more sanctified undertaking, to raise a Christian Seminary where God's holy name may ever be blessed and praised." It was a simple yet moving story, which many of those in attendance were soon able to recite from memory.[2]

For Bishop Strachan there was no doubt about the founding

moment of Trinity College. "On the 1st day of January, 1850," the founder declared, "the destruction of King's College as a Christian Institution was accomplished. For on that day the Act establishing the University of Toronto, by which it was suppressed, came into place." Here for all to see was the conjunction of principles and politics that in Strachan's mind gave birth to Trinity College. His new college was founded to restore the bond between religion and education that had been broken by the secularization of King's College and the creation of the University of Toronto. What awful symmetry: the first of January 1850, the first day of the second half of the nineteenth century; it was also the Octave of Christmas, the day on which we celebrate the naming of the Lord.[3]

Less than two years later the new college building was ready to admit its first students, and this important occasion was once again marked by rituals and homilies. At eleven o'clock divine service was conducted in the college library, which was to serve as the "temporary" chapel for the next thirty years. The community then formed itself into a procession – very much like the one that had assisted at the laying of the cornerstone – and proceeded to the "Inauguration Room" just off the entrance hall of the college. All this took place in the middle of January; there was scarcely any heat in the new building, and it was one of the coldest days of that winter.[4]

Now the first students were formally admitted to Trinity College. On that day nineteen men signed the matriculation register and declared "by God's help" that they would "faithfully obey the Laws" of the college "and diligently attend to the Studies required." Their ages ranged from seventeen to thirty-two. The inauguration ceremonies, in fact, divided this entering class into two parts. There was an older group of fifteen men (aged nineteen to thirty-two) who had been preparing for ordination at the

Diocesan Theological Institute at Cobourg, a prosperous town on Lake Ontario about eighty miles east of Toronto. They became the first students to enrol in the theological course of study, and as prospective clergymen they not only swore to obey the college rules but also signed the Thirty-nine Articles of Religion. The other four students, who were much younger (aged seventeen to twenty), were entering Trinity by enrolling in arts; consequently, they were only required to declare their intention to study hard and obey the college rules. All four of them, however, would move through arts to divinity and then seek ordination. After completing these declarations and subscriptions, each student withdrew to an adjoining room, put on the cap and gown, and returned to his seat.[5] At this point the Revd Alexander Neil Bethune, the clergyman who had taught many of these students at Cobourg, formally resigned the title of Diocesan Professor of Theology, which was then bestowed on the Revd George Whitaker, professor of divinity and the first provost of Trinity College. Both Whitaker and Bethune, who was also the archdeacon of York, played major roles in the founding and early history of Trinity College.[6]

The occasion gave Bishop Strachan another opportunity to explain the significance of what was taking place, and to repeat the founding story he had told at the laying of the cornerstone, but with some notable embellishments. As before he began with King's College. The opening of King's, he recalled, had been "the happiest moment of my life." Such happiness, however, would be short-lived. King's was "ruthlessly assailed" and then completely suppressed "before the termination of its seventh year." At this point, however, it was no longer necessary to call for the creation of a new King's College, for what had been only a cherished hope had now assumed a real presence in brick and stone. So the Bishop ascended to a grand spiritual plain, ennobling the new college in the romantic language of self-sacrifice and religious principle.

When King's College was destroyed it became "incumbent on us to sacrifice endowment rather than principle; it was impossible for us, great as the sacrifice might be, to hold connexion with an Institution essentially anti-Christian ... It became a matter of necessity, as well as duty, to establish a University from our private resources, in close connexion with the Church to which we had the happiness to belong." Trinity College, which scarcely moments before had admitted its first students, had now become, under God's superintending providence, the instrument for righting an "unexampled oppression." Alluding to one of his favorite Biblical texts (Romans 8:28–31), he reassured his audience that for them that love the Lord all things – even the most untoward – do work together for good: "Trinity College is a burst of Christian benevolence, to remedy an intolerable act of injustice, and prove that all oppression is short-sighted, and sure in God's own time to be overruled for good."

In these episodes the image of John Strachan begins to assume a new form. Long remembered as the great foe of liberalism and the unrelenting defender of unjust Anglican privileges – John Charles Dent denounced him as the great "Protestant Pope"[7] – Strachan now appears in the trappings of an old and noble warrior, prepared to defend a sacred religious principle to the death. He was so committed to the bond between religion and education that he willingly sacrificed all he had attained rather than yield to the apparent seductions of a secular world. Bishop Strachan was now a knight errant on a grand religious quest, and Trinity College had embraced its founding story, the myth of its own creation.[8]

Like all good creation stories, this account of the founding of Trinity College is a straightforward narrative. It tells a story of loss and restoration, of evil overcome by good. It reduces the history of the "university question" – without doubt one of the most complicated and tortuous stories in all of Canadian history[9] – to a simple syllogism: the secularization of King's College explains the creation of Trinity. And it is a story that leaves no doubt about the meaning of good and evil: on the one side are King's College, Trinity College, God, and true education; on the other the University of Toronto, open infidelity, liberalism, and anarchy. The authority of this myth increased with its telling. The founder himself repeated the story at every opportunity; it would be copied out in a fine round hand in the minute book of corporation (with a shorter version placed prominently in the new college calendar); it would be brought out to sustain appeals for financial support; and it would serve as the organizing framework for the first history of the college (published in 1852) – and then dutifully repeated in every subsequent account of the college's creation.[10]

In creating such a story, this small Anglican college in a rather remote part of the British Empire was participating in an essential and universal cultural act. All nations and peoples rely on such founding stories to secure their identities, define a sense of time and place, and bind themselves together as distinct communities. Indeed the power and importance of such stories give them a life of their own; they prosper in an atmosphere of faith and memory that seems largely immune from critical analysis. And yet the one hundred and fiftieth anniversary of the founding of Trinity College presents a unique opportunity to revisit this founding moment – to step behind the received wisdom of the founder's story and draw out some of the deeper historical and cultural themes that shaped the creation of this important institution.

On the surface the basic elements of the founding story seem beyond dispute. King's College *was* suppressed, the University of Toronto *did* reject any official religious creed, and Trinity *was* established as a church university in which religion figured prominently, indeed dominated almost every aspect of college life. And yet in telling this story the founder was also indulging in some very creative misdirection. Like a fine illusionist, he drew the attention of those before him to a single issue while concealing what was going on elsewhere in his grand performance. Certain things were meant to be seen; others were not. In this way the prominence accorded to the founding story has relegated other, and often very significant, issues to the shadows of our historical memory.

Let us begin with what was at the very heart of Strachan's founding story – the relationship between King's College and Trinity. As we have noted, Strachan asserted continually that Trinity was restoring what had been lost with the secularization of King's College: that Trinity was King's reborn.[11] But the connection between these two colleges was in fact much more tenuous; indeed in many ways they were two very different institutions. King's College was a public university, richly endowed with public land, that formed an integral part of the Upper Canadian state system.[12] Trinity College was a private university, supported almost entirely from private sources, and it purposefully distanced itself from the new state system. More important, the single irrefutable fact that appears to bind these two institutions together, that King's and Trinity were both "church universities," proves upon closer analysis to have in fact pulled the two colleges apart. For, although King's and Trinity were both "church" institutions and although both prepared candidates for ordination, the church to which King's had been attached was very different from the one to which Trinity was to be so intimately connected.[13]

To appreciate this critical matter of ecclesiastical polity we must revisit briefly that "abominable incubus," the changing relationship between church and state in English Canada in the middle of the nineteenth century.[14] During the formative years of King's College, the Anglican Church (the United Church of England and Ireland) had been engaged in a protracted battle to defend its position as the established church in the colony. The church saw itself as an ally of the state, and this alliance shaped in turn both the ideology and the practices of the colonial church.[15] By the terms of this "civil" or "mutual compact," the state was to provide the church with the protection and financial support it required to carry out its religious mission. And in carrying out this mission, the church was also serving the larger interests of the state. For by making the people of Upper Canada into good Christians, the church was also making them into loyal and faithful subjects of the crown and providing the social order that the state needed but could not attain on its own. Within this alliance the church was, in effect, a public institution providing a public good. The clergy were like a primitive civil service working through the state to bring the blessings of salvation (and order) to every inhabitant of the colony. The church needed the state in order to fulfill its religious function; the state needed the church in order to ensure public order. Once again all things worked together for good.

The Revd C.B. Gribble, an Anglican missionary in Dunnville, Canada West, summarized the basic assumptions of the alliance between church and state in a letter to the Society for the Propagation of the Gospel: "Our principles teach men to be good subjects on religious grounds, the government will therefore do right to help forward our principles. And they will therefore do what is expedient[,] for the principles of the church, where followed up by a faithful clergyman, beget humility and submission, order and peace."[16] Bishop Strachan made the same point, but more bluntly: "A Christian nation without a religious establishment is a contradiction."[17]

In order to carry out this religious and social task, however, the church had to appeal to a wide spectrum, to try to make itself synonymous with the nation itself. For this reason the church had to avoid restrictive creeds and keep its religious tests to a minimum.

It needed to bring dissenters back to the church, not turn them away. "A great church," explained John Travers Lewis, the first bishop of Ontario, "cannot have narrow tests. A happy characteristic of our Church is the slight interference with the private opinions of her members, and however varied may be those opinions, it is consolatory to know that men are never so good or so bad as their opinions."[18] In effect the church had to walk a political and administrative tightrope – defending its privileged position as a colonial establishment while trying to broaden its appeal in order to gather into the church as many groups as possible.

The tension between protection and inclusion runs right through the history of King's College. King's was essential to the present and future life of the colonial church, for not only would it train future generations of colonial clergymen (at very little cost to the church), but it would also instill in all its graduates the deference to authority and respect for order that were at the centre of the political and social philosophy that sustained both the church and the state.[19] For this reason Strachan fought hard to protect the position of the church within the provincial university. Indeed, the battle for King's College was at this moment even more critical because the colonial religious establishment – albeit in an attenuated form – seemed on the verge of actually becoming a functioning and beneficial reality. In the mid-1840s not only had King's College opened its doors, but the clergy reserves – that second cornerstone of the colonial establishment – were actually producing revenue. For the first time there was a surplus that promised in a few years to grow into enough income to sustain a full programme of rapid church expansion.

It was not enough, however, just to defend King's College. For King's to perform its function in the colonial establishment, it had to appeal to as many groups as possible and reach well beyond an exclusively Anglican constituency to convince other religious groups that the college was worthy of broad public support. Consequently, the church tried to minimize its position in the college. The charter granted to King's was considered one of the most liberal instruments of the day; and it is widely acknowledged that John Strachan (who was then archdeacon of York) had lobbied to have the presence of the Anglican Church in the new college reduced even further.[20] Certainly the revisions made to the Royal Charter in 1837 reaffirmed and expanded upon the inclusive assumptions that were central to establishment thinking. Thus King's imposed no denominational tests on students either entering or graduating from the college. All manner of students were welcome. Although there was an Anglican professor of divinity, the only religious test imposed on the faculty and college council was a simple declaration that "they believe in the authenticity and Divine inspiration of the Old and New Testaments, and in the doctrine of the Trinity." Only deists and unitarians were sent scurrying for cover. Though chapel services were an important part of the life of King's College, students who were not Anglican were not required to attend.[21] In effect, King's was a church institution in that the United Church of England and Ireland was accorded official status, but the influence of the church was purposefully limited, and dissenters were reassured that while religion was an important part of higher education, the presence of the church in general and Anglican religious practices in particular would not give offence to the religious views of non-Anglican parents and their children.[22]

This broad, inclusive strategy was sustained by the political realities of the day. It must be remembered that the place of religion and the church had always been the flash point in the political battles that surrounded King's College. Almost all the religious denominations, including many Anglicans, challenged the privileged position of the church, however reduced that position might be. Once again Strachan had to minimize the role of the church, and when opponents attacked the few privileges the church still enjoyed, he was prepared to reduce the church's role even further in order to broaden the appeal of the college and protect the place of King's in the colonial establishment.

Here Robert Baldwin may well be thanked for his surgical skill in cutting through decades of compromise and concession by simply removing the Anglican Church – indeed any church – from the provincial university. But in taking this dramatic step Baldwin was also undermining the entire establishment position that had sustained the church's hopes and ambitions. What point was there in still defending a university in which the church now had no place? Why try to reconcile dissent within a university that was no longer part of the colonial religious establishment? Baldwin's Act became Strachan's own Rubicon. With its passage he now began to decry the secularization of King's, attack the godless University of Toronto, call for the creation of Trinity College, and seek a way to wrest the church itself from the grasp of his former ally.

Baldwin's Act had another important outcome. By forcing the church out of the university and destroying an essential part of the connection between church and state, the Act made it inevitable that the new church college would be placed in an entirely different context. King's was a public university where religious tests were so inclusive that they were almost meaningless in the broadly Christian community of Canada West. King's welcomed dissenters and celebrated their accomplishments.[23] Trinity College, in marked contrast, was a private university, completely separated from the state, and it was to be (in Strachan's own words) "strictly a Church of England institution."[24] Severe religious tests were imposed on the college council, all members of every faculty (arts, divinity, law, and medicine), and every student. In effect, at Trinity College one had to be Anglican to govern, to teach, or to take a degree. Chapel services at Trinity were conducted according to the *Book of Common Prayer*, and chapel services were frequent and compulsory – even those students who were given a provostial dispensation to live with their parents were required to arrive at the college before nine every morning in time for Morning Prayer.[25]

It is also clear that Strachan's attack on the University of Toronto should not be taken at face value. Without doubt the last vestiges of the church had been removed, but Toronto was far from the godless institution that the Bishop liked to portray. Religion remained firmly rooted in the new university; indeed the new university quickly took steps to reaffirm its presence.[26] Although students no longer studied divinity they were obliged to take courses in natural theology (one of the few requirements all students had to fulfil). Here they learned how nature, if rightly understood, confirmed the existence and benevolence of a divine intelligence, and prestigious prizes were awarded to students who excelled in this subject.[27] And to Strachan's great embarrassment this subject was taught at the Toronto university by the Revd James Beaven, the one-time professor of divinity at King's College, who had survived without apparent moral injury the transition to Toronto and godlessness. He became professor of metaphysics and ethics at the University of Toronto, where he remained, despite Strachan's efforts to get him out of the Diocese of Toronto, until 1871.[28]

There was also the gnawing fact that several prominent Anglicans had taken an active part in the founding and early years of the University of Toronto. Among them were Robert Baldwin, Peter Boyle De Blaquiere (the first chancellor), and the Revd John McCaul. McCaul was an Anglican cleryman one-time principal of Upper Canada College (or the Minor College), and Strachan's successor as the president of King's College. He seemed to prosper under secularization, becoming the first president of the University of Toronto, and with the reorganization of the university in 1853, the first president of University College, a post he held until his retirement in 1880.[29] When the matter of godlessness is seen in this light, Strachan's claims appear greatly exaggerated. However heretical it may seem, the true successor to King's was not Trinity College, but the University of Toronto. For if one examines the link between religion and education, which was Strachan's primary concern, one discovers that at King's and Toronto the same amount of religion was taught to the same students by the same people.[30] In fact, the founders of the University of Toronto marked the continuity by carving the phrase *olim collegii regalis* into the stone that commemorates the opening of their fine building.

But the charge that the new University of Toronto was a place where God could not be found proved very useful for Strachan the politician. If the presence of the Anglican Church had been the Achilles heel of King's College, Strachan quickly understood that the absence of a church (and the apparent absence of religion) was the Achilles heel of the new University of Toronto. Methodists and Presbyterians may have opposed Anglican privileges at King's, but they were deeply suspicious of Baldwin's new Act. Consequently, as John Moir has pointed out, Strachan's critique of the University of Toronto fell on fertile ground, winning him some very powerful allies. Both Victoria and Queen's refused to give up their charters and join the new provincial leviathan, and their refusal set a pattern: for the rest of the nineteenth century, Ontario was to enjoy a system in which private church colleges competed with a public non-denominational one – or as the University of Toronto liked to put it, there was a single national university and several small outlying colleges.[31]

The fact that the official founding story of Trinity College relies to a considerable degree on such creative misdirection does not, however, reduce the significance of this founding moment, of what was actually taking place on the first day of January, 1850. Trinity may not have been quite what the founder had claimed, but the founding of Trinity is nevertheless a very important event. It marks a watershed in the history of the church; it reveals a new representation of the relationship between religion and public life; and it illuminates an important episode in the history of Canadian higher education. But only by stepping behind this founding story can we see the important social, cultural, religious, and institutional themes that inform this founding moment. To do this, let us return to that grand procession that was making its way along Queen Street, from the Church of St George the Martyr to Gore Vale, the site of the new Trinity College. Here we see a well-crafted public event filled with cultural meaning – an event that calls out to us to reflect with care and imagination on the birth of the college that was being celebrating.

First of all the urban geography of the procession is very suggestive. The site the procession approached was at the western edge of the city, long regarded as the most healthy and socially attractive part of Toronto. Strachan had built his own "palace" to the west of the town in 1818, and over the following decades this part of the city became home to a number of important public institutions, such as Osgoode Hall, Upper Canada College, and the provincial parliament. More recently the new mental asylum, one of the most ambitious and impressive public buildings ever to grace the city's streets, had just been completed to the west of the site of the new college. In contrast, when a new jail was needed a few years later, it was built to the east of the city, beside the Don River.[32]

The route the procession followed reinforced these important social and class considerations. In 1793, shortly after arriving at his new provincial capital, Lieutenant-Governor John Graves Simcoe had divided the lands along the north side of Queen, or

Lot Street as it was then called, into narrow park lots, which he then bestowed as "doceurs" upon government officials (including of course the rector of the new parish of St James) in order to make the transition from the former provincial capital at Niagara as painless as possible. Although this residential line of colonial officialdom had been thinned considerably by death and real estate speculation, Queen Street was still associated with the social and political elite with whom the new college associated itself. The procession began in front of the Grange (the home of the Bolton family) and soon passed by Beverley House (the home of the Robinsons); a little farther along was the Denison estate at Bellevue and nearer to the college site, just a short distance up Bathurst Street was "the Hall," Sir Casimir Gzowski's villa. By building on the one of these park lots the college was in effect placing itself at the end of a line that reached through the Family Compact back to founding elite of the colony.[33]

The specific site the bishop had chosen – some twenty acres at the western edge of settlement – seemed to many contemporaries to be an especially fine choice. The bishop himself opined that "it is considered, by every person capable of forming a correct judgment, to be the most beautiful and convenient for the purpose that could have been selected."[34] Trinity was to be a residential college, and Strachan wanted a site that was at some distance from the temptations of the city. There was also the innate beauty of the site and the possibilities it offered for constructing romantic and historical associations. To the south it offered a "commanding" view of Lake Ontario and Toronto Harbour. This view was enhanced by the flowing stream that had cut a deep ravine – the "elmy dale" – through the college property as it meandered away to the south and east, reaching the lake below the guns of the old fort. Future generations waxed eloquent on this brooklet – Henry Scadding finding in it "the Cephissus of a

Canadian Academus, the Cherwell of an infant Christ Church."[35] Unfortunately, its name in real life – the Garrison Creek – never seemed to live up to such romantic associations, and unlike the waters passing through Christ Church meadow, this colonial watercourse was too shallow for the racing of boats.

On the east side, the only apparent threat to these Arcadian environs was the presence of two breweries that almost abutted the college property. One of these, founded by Thomas Baines in 1844, would enjoy a long life (and close relationship with the college). In 1865 it began its long association with the Cosgrave family, not to be confused with a future Provost of the same name, and continued in operation, under various names, for almost a century.[36] Archival records reveal that its pale ale, mild ale, and extra stout found a ready market among the men of college; in fact the college (taken together) drank some 100 gallons of ale a month.[37] Why the bishop of Toronto and the other dignitaries who spoke on such occasions did not remark upon the advantages of placing the college so near to such an establishment remains one of the mysteries in the founding of Trinity College. But can one doubt that for many a man it was this conjunction of knowledge and thirst that confirmed in his mind the wisdom of the founder's decision?[38]

Some seventy years later, when Trinity College abandoned the Queen Street site for its present location on Hoskin Avenue, this part of the city had become a very different place. By the last decade of the century no fewer than six major railway lines had been built between the college gates and the lake, drawing many large industrial enterprises, such as the Massey-Harris farm machinery factory, as well as the cottages of the industrial working class. A reformatory and a prison had also joined the neighbourhood. All the while the well-to-do were abandoning the west end and taking up residence on Jarvis and Sherbourne streets, or

in the new and exclusively residential suburbs north of Bloor
Street such as Rosedale, the Annex, and Seaton Village, where in
1884 the church had acquired land on Howland Avenue to build
the new Cathedral Church of St Alban the Martyr, rejecting
another site near Trinity College.[39]

And yet those who made the decision in 1851 to build the college on Queen Street had every reason to believe that this part of
the city would remain in a bucolic and privileged state for some
time. To the south of the college and stretching well to the east
was the garrison reserve, a substantial remnant of the vast tract of
land set aside in 1793 by Simcoe for military purposes.[40] These
lands, which in 1833 still stretched from Peter Street to the Humber River, were coming under increasing pressure from urban
expansion, and perhaps with this trend in mind the City of Toronto in 1848 leased 287 acres of the remaining reserve lands, across
from the site of the college, for a new public park. Other plans
dating from this period would have added a museum and botan-
ical gardens to this site. The lease was to run for 999 years, and
if these plans had been completed, Trinity College would have
been on the edge of one of the finest public spaces in the entire
city, and the western suburbs might well have continued to be
regarded as the most healthy and beautiful part of the city. Unfortunately for the College (and the citizens of the city), the military
authorities revoked the lease in 1852, claiming that it needed the
land for pensioners' housing. Such housing, however, was never
built, and the reserve was soon given over to commercial and residential development.[41]

The composition of the procession that followed this route to
the site of the new college can also help us to understand other
important (and largely unexamined) aspects of the founding of
Trinity College. Near the head of the procession we see the pupils
of St Paul's Church Grammar School holding aloft their banner

proclaiming "In Cruce Salus. Nil Sine Episcopo."[42] A similar group of students (and their masters) would also form part of the procession that marked the inauguration ceremonies in January 1852. The prominence given to students at both these founding rituals alerts us to a problem facing the founders. They knew that the success of their undertaking depended to a considerable degree upon the college's ability to attract enough qualified students. Consequently, they set about trying to link Trinity directly to church grammar schools, which taught the classical curriculum that prepared the students for the matriculation examination. These schools would then feed students into Trinity College and in time provide employment for its graduates, both clerical and lay. With this end in view, the new college council at one of its first meetings passed a resolution setting out the terms on which church grammar schools could affiliate with their new college; and in return for "union," the graduates of these grammar schools would be given preference when they applied for admission to the college. The first such school to take advantage of this provision was St Paul's Church Grammar School.[43]

This concern with grammar schools and enrolments was one that John Strachan knew well. He had been the master of two renowned grammar schools, which by his own humble measure had prepared a generation of young men to assume positions of influence in colonial society. Then, as president of the General Board of Education, he had overseen the first attempt in the colony to develop a broad state-supported system of schooling, which included common schools, district grammar schools, and in time a university. Strachan had also been intimately involved in the birth and early history of Upper Canada College. This was the grammar school Sir John Colborne had founded to meet what he regarded as the most pressing educational need in the colony. Modelled on a school that he knew on the Island of Guernsey, this *soi-disant* Eton was intended to train the sons of the local elite and prepare them to enter King's College, whose opening had in fact been delayed by the founding of Upper Canada College. The Council of King's College, however, was given responsibility for Upper Canada in 1833, and in 1839 it was also entrusted with the supervision of all state-supported grammar schools in the colony. In effect, as president of King's College, Strachan was able to exercise a large measure of control over both King's and the schools that would prepare students to enter the college.[44]

From this perspective, allying Trinity College to a group of grammar schools can be seen as a strategy for reproducing in a new situation the relationship between King's College, Upper Canada College, and the district grammar schools. But there was one major difference. Whereas King's College, Upper Canada, and the district grammar schools were all, in various ways, supported by the state (endowed with crown lands or provided with government grants), the grammar schools that Trinity appealed to did not receive state support. Indeed, the terms on which grammar schools could apply for union with Trinity – they were required to provide testimonials that the schools offered systematic instruction in the doctrines of the church and "that the Head Master and regular assistants [were] Members of that Church"[45] – specifically precluded them from receiving the grants that the government gave to other grammar schools in the province. In effect, we see much the same story being played out at the grammar-school level that we saw with the founding of Trinity College. In the same way that Trinity had to step outside the state system (and lose the endowment of King's), so the grammar schools with which Trinity sought affiliation would have to survive outside the charmed circle of state support – and like Trinity these church grammar schools would now demand a level of doctrinal orthodoxy that had never been required in the state-supported system.[46]

This strategy, however, was largely a failure. Only two church grammar schools were accepted into union with Trinity College, and neither of these appears to have survived long enough to provide much benefit to the college. Furthermore, the old system of state-supported grammar schools (to which the college also appealed for students) was reorganized in the 1870s and brought into a new secondary level of high schools and collegiate institutes.[47] And once this restructured system of public education was in place, it seemed determined, at least in the eyes of the supporters of Trinity College, to point its students towards the University of Toronto, passing over Trinity College both as a place to educate its graduates and as a source of teachers for its own schools.[48]

Having failed to create a system of church grammar schools, Trinity College modified its strategy for acquiring students. It agreed to support the creation of a new type of church school, an Anglican boarding school for boys, which then affiliated directly with the college.[49] In 1857 the college began its long and tortuous relationship with Trinity College School, which in spite of the persistent threat of financial entanglements, prepared a small but steady stream of students for its parent institution. In future years this association was expanded into an informal alliance with all the major private schools in the province. This important founding theme is reflected in the oriel window in Strachan Hall, which contains the crests of the old grammar schools (Cornwall, Jarvis, and Galt) and the boys' private schools – Trinity College School, Upper Canada, Bishop Ridley, Appleby, Ashbury, and St Andrew's.

A little farther along in the procession we see the members of the Faculties of Arts, Medicine, Law, and Divinity as well as the "students in medicine"; the presence of these groups reveals another important and largely neglected aspect of the founding of Trinity College. When Trinity federated with the University of Toronto in 1904, it brought two faculties into the university, Arts and Divinity, and this fact has erased the memory of the professional faculties, most notably medicine, that did not survive federation. And yet the first lectures in Trinity College were in neither arts nor divinity; rather they were given by the members of the newly formed Faculty of Medicine. On 7 November 1850, more than a year before the college opened, Dr Francis Badgley, professor of the practice of medicine, lectured on "medical jurisprudence"; he was followed by Drs Hodder, Bethune, Hallowell, Melville, and Bovell, who lectured on obstetrics, anatomy, materia medica, surgery, and medical practice respectively. The lectures were held in the Mechanics Institute.[50] It is also important to point out that the medical faculty enjoyed considerable independence within the governing structure (most likely the result of a rift between faculty and Provost Whitaker), and for many years enrolment in the medical school exceeded the combined enrolment in all other parts of the college.[51]

The presence of these professional groups also draws us further into the social and class assumptions that were at the heart of the founding vision of Trinity College. Indeed on this point Bishop Strachan spoke candidly and forcefully. In a colony like Upper Canada, he argued, where there was no landed aristocracy, it was the members of the learned professions – clergy, physicians, and especially lawyers – who would assume positions of power and constitute the new social and political elite.[52] These "professional gentlemen," as Bob Gidney and Wyn Millar have shown, were set apart by their "regular opinions" (the attitudes they shared about their professions), their privileged social position, and their place in the new state system.[53] The university would not only "train" these groups – instructing them in how to hector, how to pettifog, and how to cut with a knife – it would also bring these groups together and cultivate within its collegiate atmosphere those social and cultural values that, in effect, would bind together this

new social and political elite. In this way Trinity College was supposed to play a crucial role in the process of class and state formation.[54] It almost goes without saying that this new elite would
be tied to Trinity College, and over time college graduates would
move effortlessly into this most privileged of social ranks. And
this was one of the true cornerstones of Strachan's philosophy of
education. A university education not only imparted knowledge
and skill; it also bestowed professional authority and social status. The university degree was not merely an academic marker; it
also proclaimed one's class position.

At the same time, Bishop Strachan was trying his best to mark
these professional gentlemen in one other important way. King's
College, as we have already noted, did not place any denominational or credal requirements on its graduates; nor were there any
religious tests for membership in the learned professions. (A
church, of course, could impose such a test at ordination.) But the
founders believed that the church had a role in professional, and
especially medical, training, and they were prepared to impose
religious tests on everyone studying for the professions at Trinity
College. To teach at Trinity, including medicine, one had to subscribe to the articles of religion; to take a degree one had to be a
member of the church. In effect, every clergyman, doctor, and
lawyer that Trinity produced had to be a member of the Anglican
Church. Here again the church was trying to assert a place for
itself in public life. The world of professional gentlemen had no
religious tests, but within this world there would be a distinct
group of professional gentlemen tied to the Anglican Church.

It was on this very point that the first sustained challenge was
launched against the founding vision of Trinity College. The
Anglican physicians who had founded a medical faculty quickly
realized that it was economically and professionally impossible to
run a medical school along strictly Anglican lines, that is, to insist

that all the students and all the professors be members of the Anglican Church. In 1856, when Provost Whitaker refused to give way on this point, the members of the medical faculty resigned en masse. And the medical school only returned to the college some fifteen years later when a modus vivendi was reached allowing medical students and faculty to apply for a dispensation from the religious tests that the college still applied to everyone else.[55] Trinity then became a church college with a medical school that trained doctors without regard to their denominational affiliation. They entered their profession as doctors trained by the Trinity Medical School, not as doctors who were necessarily members of the Anglican Church.

In the procession another group of aspiring professional gentlemen followed close behind the students in medicine. Here we see "the students in Divinity," a group whose presence should surprise no one. The training of clergy for the church was always central to Bishop Strachan's vision of a university, and he had proclaimed this role for King's College from the moment of that college's inception.[56] But there was something particular about this group of divinity students. Most of them had begun their preparation for the church at the Diocesan Theological Institute in Cobourg under Archdeacon Bethune. Those who had not yet completed the course at the institute transferred to Trinity and became the first divinity class at the new college, and at the inauguration ceremony they were the first students to sign the matriculation register.

On this score Bishop Strachan's account of the history of the college has done particular damage to our appreciation of the founding moment. Strachan, of course, represented Trinity as the true successor to King's College, but in truth many of the origins of Trinity are to be found, not in King's, but in this small theological seminary that had grown up and prospered in Cobourg.

Even a partial list of these connections places the matter of parenthood beyond doubt. Both Trinity and the Diocesan Theological Institute were private church institutions, the institute presented Trinity with its first students, the financial grant given to the institute by the Society for the Propagation of the Gospel provided the core funding for Trinity College, the scholarships the Society gave to the students in Cobourg were taken over by Trinity, and at least two parts of the curriculum of Trinity – classics and Divinity – were undertaken at the Diocesan Theological Institute. Just as important, much of the early student culture at Trinity (most notably the Literary Institute and the playing of cricket) was brought to Toronto by the students who had begun their academic studies at Cobourg.[57]

Indeed the connection between these two institutions became almost absolute. The Diocesan Theological Institute had begun as a small, unnamed seminary in 1841; to Strachan its existence was merely a temporary expedient for the training of clergy until King's College was operating.[58] By the late 1840s, however, this small seminary had become a thriving enterprise, and Strachan and Bethune began to consider transforming it into a proper college by increasing enrolment, adding science and mathematics to the curriculum, and putting up a college building. To enhance this change in status Bishop Strachan also set about trying to raise Bethune's academic profile by finding him an honorary degree. He appealed on Bethune's behalf to his old friend in Scotland, the Revd Thomas Duncan at St Andrew's, explaining that Bethune has always been "to me as a son [and] has no academical or university degree."[59] It is fascinating to note that the name he proposed for this expanded seminary at Cobourg was Trinity College – the first time the founder used this name. If Strachan had pursued this course Trinity might well have entered this world as an expanded seminary in the town of Cobourg, and might have rivaled at close range the Methodist Victoria College, which was just up the hill.[60]

By almost any measure Cobourg was an extraordinary success.[61] Close to eighty students attended the institute, and sixty-nine of them were ordained. It also managed to do all this (unlike Trinity College) at very little cost. But it was not able confer on its graduates the one thing Bishop Strachan was most determined to have. He wanted his clergy to be professional gentlemen, to far exceed the level of accomplishments required by the dissenting denominations, and to have the social position and authority that would win them the respect and allegiance of their congregations. To this end he insisted that all his clergy should have a bachelor's degree. But Cobourg did not offer degrees; so he closed the Diocesan Theological Institute, created a faculty of divinity within a university, and drew up a curriculum in which students would earn their Bachelor of Arts degrees before proceeding to the theological course of study. It is also instructive to note that the first group of men to receive academic degrees from Trinity College by special dispensation were clergy who had completed their training at Cobourg before Trinity opened its doors. In effect Strachan was trying bring these Cobourg graduates up to this new standard of theological formation by giving them a bachelor's degree.[62]

The relationship between Cobourg and Trinity also helps to place the founding of Trinity in a broader imperial church context. Strachan's founding story situates Trinity within a debate over secularization, for the college was founded to protect the link between religion and education. The Diocesan Theological Institute, however, was a response to the search for new ways to train clergy at a time when the traditional methods no longer met the needs of a changing social order. In Britain this concern took the form of a critique of the old universities, which in the eyes of their critics did not offer either the theological or the practical training that was necessary for an increasingly urban and industrial society. This issue, which cut across party lines, led to the creation or expansion both of Tractarian seminaries, such as those at Wells and Chichester, and of evangelical institutions, such as St Bees, Cumbria; St John's, Highbury; and St Aidan's, Birkenhead. And in the Diocese of Toronto, the institute at Cobourg was created in order to correct what Strachan saw as the shortcomings in the two sources of clergymen he had relied on up to this point: apprenticeship to older clergymen or importing of ready-made clergymen from abroad.[63]

Bishop Strachan, of course, was keenly interested in the debates that were taking place in Britain over the proper place for theological training, and his decision to close the Diocesan Theological Institute and create a faculty of divinity in a complete university represents not only an affirmation of the need for a university degree, but also a rejection of the most popular Tractarian means of clerical training at that time – separate diocesan seminaries that trained university graduates for ordination.

Strachan, however, was especially taken by a fascinating experiment in theological education at Birkenhead near Liverpool. Here an evangelical seminary, St Aidan's, was being transformed from a small seminary into much more substantial academic institution. It was strongly supported by the church and largely financed from private sources. When Strachan was in Britain raising money for Trinity College, he must have sought out this experiment, which in so many ways paralleled what he was trying to accomplish in Toronto. He was impressed enough with St Aidan's to return to Toronto with the plan for the new college building. He then gave the plan to the architects who were competing for the contract to design the new Trinity College. The similarity between St Aidan's, Birkenhead, and Kivas Tully's successful design for Trinity College is obvious.[64]

And yet once it was completed the new college building was given very different architectural associations. This fascinating link between Trinity and the search for new methods of clerical training in Britain was effectively buried as the founders pushed the limits of architectural appreciation to describe the new Trinity College building in the language of the Gothic revival and tie Trinity to the colleges of Oxford and Cambridge – the very institutions the founding of these new church colleges had set out to remedy:

> The building is designed in the Third Period of Pointed English Architecture, or that style which prevailed in the latter part of the fourteenth and the beginning of the fifteenth centuries, when the independence of the Anglo-Catholic Church was restored and the great principles of the Reformation promulgated, about which time Pointed Architecture, which had previously been applied to the construction of ecclesiastical edifices, was first introduced in the erection of buildings not strictly ecclesiastical; and, as the colleges of England are considered the best specimens of its introduction, it may be appropriately termed the Collegiate Style.[65]

But the language of the Gothic revival, however jarring architecturally, was necessary to the story Bishop Strachan was trying to tell. Trinity was to be born with a tradition; it did not want to be accused of anything new and creative. It was intended to restore, not to innovate. Consequently the building was described in words and phrases that linked Trinity to the ancient colleges of England.

There was one other group in the procession that must have impressed everyone in attendance. The procession was distinguished by a very large number of clergy. Close to one hundred had attended the special service in the Church of St George the Martyr that preceded the march to Gore Vale, and almost all of them appear to have joined the procession to the site of the new college. Clergy, of course, were a fixture at many public events, their presence proclaiming their own status as well as the position of the church in the colonial establishment. But on this occasion their numbers were unlike anything the city had seen, and their presence marked another important theme in the founding of Trinity College and the history of the Canadian church.

Here we must look forward to what took place on the day following the laying of the cornerstone. On 1 May 1850, Strachan was to open a very special convocation.[66] It was his custom every third year to invite all his clergy to Toronto for his triennial visitation – in the other two years he would travel first to the east and then to the west, visiting every parish in his extensive diocese. On this occasion, however, Strachan took a step that would drastically change the character of the Canadian church. He invited the clergy to bring one or two lay members of their congregations with them to share in their deliberations. This became, in effect, the first meeting of the synod of the Diocese of Toronto, although the legal status of diocesan synods had to wait on a long series of legal appeals that reached all the way to the Judicial Committee of the Privy Council.[67]

The juxtaposition of the laying of the cornerstone of Trinity College and the meeting of the first synod of the Diocese of Toronto speaks volumes about the significance of these two events. The demise of the Anglican religious establishment, marked here by the removal of the church from the provincial university, had left Strachan with the worst of all possible worlds. The state was no longer prepared to live up to its part of the alliance – to provide for and protect the church – but it still controlled large elements of the church's life, including the power of presentment to the rectories that the crown had endowed in 1836. In effect the diocesan synod became the main instrument in an institutional revolution through which the church gained the ability to determine its own affairs. It became the cornerstone of the new Canadian church. This was not the broad, public church of the old colonial establishment; rather it was a private church administered by an exclusively Anglican body made up of the clergy, the bishop, and the laity.

The elaborate ceremonies that marked the founding of Trinity College tell the same story. King's College, like the old church, was a public institution built at a public site. But Trinity, like the new church, was a private institution built at a private site. Indeed the procession that advanced along Queen Street was this new church college on parade, with its complex of social and cultural attitudes revealed in its composition and progress. Indeed, when seen in this light, the grand procession has one final secret to reveal. The transition from the old state church to the new denomination, from the old university to the new college, is also marked by who is missing from this rich social and cultural tableau. At the laying of the cornerstone of King's College, the state was prominently on display – here we find the vice-regal personage, the government officials, and the military – "a full representation of all the National and other Societies, Public Bodies and Public Functionaries."[68] Guns were fired to salute this important state occasion. But at the founding moment of Trinity the church and the college marched alone: the state was remarkable only for its absence; as in the mystery of Silver Blaze, it was the dog that did not bark.

Here we return again to Strachan's founding story. By linking King's and Trinity, Strachan was not only making a political and a religious claim; he was also embedding Trinity within a tradition. Trinity College would always be Old Trinity, orthodox and catholic, restoring a line that, the first history of the college claimed, stretched back through King's College through the ancient universities of Britain to the first universities in Paris and

Bologna. Trinity came into the world bound up in some thousand years of religious and educational history. But the language of restoration and tradition disguised what was really a very radical and decisive act. Trinity was a new university that was part of a new Church of God setting out to minister to a new and changing world.

Where the procession began: The Church of St George the Martyr, Toronto

The destination: The "elmy dale"

Fundator noster: Portrait of Bishop Strachan by G. T. Berthon

"Faithfully obey the Laws thereof, and diligently attend to the Studies required of me." The matriculation register

Creating history: Sketch of King's College by Catherine Beaven (n.d.)

Rob. Baldwin

Drawn by H. Meyer

The villain of the piece: Portrait of Robert Baldwin by Hoppner
Francis Meyer (1845)

"A gorgeous temple of infidelity"

Above: Construction of the east wing of University College (c. 1858)

Right: University College from the southeast (c. 1870) (Cumberland & Storm, architects)

Two who stayed on

Above: The Revd John McCaul, last president of King's College and first president of the University of Toronto

Left: The Revd James Beaven, professor of divinty, King's College and professor of metaphysics and ethics, University of Toronto

Thirst and knowledge: Receipted payment for 90 gallons of ale,
Cosgrave & Sons, 8 December 1877

Acquiring the appropriate students: The banner
of St Paul's Church Grammar School

The importance of the professions: The constitution of the medical faculty of Trinity College

Another founder: Portrait of the Revd
Alexander Neil Bethune by Théophile Hamel

Another parent: The Diocesan Theological Institute, Cobourg
(Henry Bowyer Lane, architect, c. 1841)

The founder's proposed design: St Aidan's College, Birkenhead
(Wyatt & Brandon, architects, c. 1850)

Trinity College, front elevation (Kivas Tully, architect, 1851)

Minutes of Proceedings at the Visitation of the Lord Bishop of Toronto,

HELD IN THE CHURCH OF THE HOLY TRINITY, TORONTO, ON THE 1st & 2nd MAY, 1851.

THURSDAY, MAY 1, 1851, *the Festival of St. Philip and St. James.*

This being the day appointed by the Lord Bishop of Toronto, in his Pastoral Letter, dated 2nd of April, 1851, for the holding of the Triennial Visitation, there was Divine Service at the Church of the Holy Trinity, Toronto, at Eleven o'clock, A. M.

Prayers were said by the Rev. E. Denroche, A. M., Incumbent of St. Peter's Church, Brockville; the Lessons were read by the Rev. Saltern Givins, Incumbent of St. Jude's Church, Oakville and Rural Dean of the Midland Deanery; the ante-Communion Service was read by the Venerable Archdeacon of York, the Rev. Saltern Givins reading the Epistle; the Sermon was preached by the Rev. W. M. Herchmer, M. A., Chaplain to the Lord Bishop, from the 2nd chapter of Malachi, 7th verse; Holy Commmunion was administered by the Lord Bishop, the Ven. the Archdeacon of Kingston, the Ven. the Archdeacon of York, and the Rev. H. J. Grasett, Domestic Chaplain to the Lord Bishop.

Divine Service being ended, the Lord Bishop stated that he would deliver his Charge at Three o'clock.

Three o'clock.

The clergy and the lay representatives from their several missions or congregations whom they had invited, at the request of the Lord Bishop, to accompany them to this Visitation, having taken their places in the Church,

Clergy and laity called together: Minutes of the proceedings at the visitation of the Lord Bishop of Toronto (1, 2 May 1851)

2

A University Worthy
of the Name

My present object therefore in writing is to request you to
select three gentlemen willing to devote themselves for some years
or longer as they please to the founding and raising up
of a University worthy of the name.
Bishop Strachan to the Revd Ernest Hawkins, 16 February 1851.[1]

The demise of King's College on the first day of January 1850 was
a watershed in the history of the Anglican Church in Canada. Up
to this point the church in the Diocese of Toronto had been driv-
en by the single dominant ambition of securing what it saw as its
rightful place as the colonial religious establishment. Working on
a number of fronts the church set out to acquire the clergy, create
the social and religious institutions, and procure the financial
resources that would allow it to join with the state in raising up a
hierarchical society founded on the Christian virtues of duty, deference to authority, and order. This strategy was bound up in a
millennial vision of the place of Upper Canada in the redemption
of the world – "for as the influence of Christian principles
extend," Strachan prophesied, "murmurs will give way to blessings and praise; and one-fourth of the human race being thus
reclaimed, the remainder will gradually follow, and thus the

whole earth become the garden of the Lord."[2]

But on this fateful day Robert Baldwin and his reform allies unceremoniously removed the church from the provincial university, depriving Strachan of the institution that was intended to play such a vital role in the church's programme of social and religious construction. And then four years later a different band of Canadian politicians (including the young John A. Macdonald) applied the same rigour to the other cornerstone of the colonial establishment, the clergy reserves. In its own words this legislation set out "to remove all semblance of connexion between church and state." The Act protected the "vested interests" of the clergy whose salaries were being paid from the reserves; they could either continue to receive their salaries from the government or "commute" their rights in return for a lump-sum payment to the church, which then assumed responsibility for paying them. At the same time the Act applied the new revenues that the reserves generated to purely secular purposes. Instead of supporting "a protestant clergy," it now underwrote municipal improvements, such as railway construction. The church had waited for decades for these lands to produce the income it needed; now it was losing what had just become its primary source of financial support.[3] With the passage of these two Acts it had become evident to even the most seasoned warrior that the battle the church had been fighting for the last fifty years was lost. Not the people, nor the state, nor the crown was prepared to tolerate a colonial religious establishment. Strachan's own appeal to Lord John Russell offers a fitting eulogy to the old Anglican vision of Upper Canada: "to speak of the Church, as in unity with the State in the present state of things is as ridiculous as it is untrue."[4]

The founding of Trinity College defined the new course the church would follow after disestablishment. Once the church had lost its position in the provincial university, it set about creating a

new church university that would be free from government interference, one that was entirely under its own control. At the same
time the church instituted a system of synodical government that
transferred effective control of the church from the colonial and
imperial state to a private religious convocation composed of the
bishop, the clergy, and representatives of the laity. Cast out of the
public sphere, the church was recreating itself at a private site, and
by 1854 the Diocese of Toronto had achieved an independence
that became the envy of the Anglican world. These two extraordinary triumphs – the freeing of the church from the state and the
achievement of self-government – were, in my estimation, Bishop
Strachan's most important and lasting contributions to the Anglican Church, although it is doubtful that he would have agreed.[5]

And yet even at this moment of triumph a number of crucial
questions still remained. The church had created a new institutional structure that was set apart from the state and firmly under
its own control; in the words of Trinity's first chancellor, it was
now able "to work out its useful purposes in peace."[6] But it was
by no means clear what these useful purposes actually were. What
kind of religion, what ideas and values, should be poured into this
new vessel? The church now had its own college, but in 1851
Trinity College was little more than an academic shell, an artifice
conjured up by a determined warrior in the midst of battle to foil
the attacks of his enemies. The college had selected a site and it
had presented two architectural firms with a drawing of an evangelical seminary on the Mersey; but as yet the college had no
faculty, no curriculum, no rules and regulations, and (most dis-
tressing of all) almost no money – and only the vaguest of promises that financial support would be forthcoming. To put the
matter another way, the church's hard won independence was at
this point an empty vessel, a form largely unencumbered by content. The church had a vision of its own college; it now had to

build that college and decide what collegiate life and culture it would pour into this new structure. Over the next few years the founders would discover what independence actually meant.

———

Two tasks had to be taken up immediately. Strachan wanted to have his university in operation as quickly as possible: "The Church ought to do nothing by halves."[7] Consequently, he quickly chose a site and then tried to reduce the time needed to prepare the plans by giving drawings of another college to the competing architects to serve as their guide.[8] And once the design was chosen, he urged the architect and the contractor to have the building ready for use on 1 October 1851, a mere five months after the laying of the cornerstone. At later times in the history of the college, temporary accommodations were used until funds and enrolments could sustain more permanent schemes.[9] At the founding of Trinity, however, this simply would not do: Strachan wanted his Gothic pile completed without delay. But pushing ahead so quickly made the second task even more imperative. Gothic dreams did not come cheap, and such large outlays for land and construction forced the founders to try to raise large sums of money at the same speed. These two themes – the constructing of the building and the raising of money to pay for it – dominated the first few years of the college's existence, and the failure of the second to keep pace with the first meant that for many decades the Arcadian tranquillity of collegiate life was always being threatened by a financial crisis.

Two administrative structures were created to carry out these tasks. On 15 April 1850 the "General Board to Promote the Interests of the Church University" met for the first time.[10] It was set up primarily as a fundraising body, and unlike other college boards and councils, this board, which soon became known as the

Church University Board was broadly representative of the colonial church, its membership being drawn from the clergy, the churchwardens, and the local committees that had been set up to support the new college. The board, which took up its mandate with considerable enthusiasm and effect, quickly extended its canvass into every parish in the diocese. Such a large board, however, did not seem as well suited to the more specialized tasks facing the college, such as purchasing the site, overseeing the construction of the building, drawing up the college statutes, developing a curriculum, and setting down the rules and regulations that would govern college life. Consequently, in January 1851 Strachan established a new "Provisional Council" made up of twelve members, six chosen by the contributors to the college and six, including a member of the medical faculty, chosen by Strachan himself. The bishop was to preside at all meetings and the two archdeacons of the diocese were to serve on the council *ex officio*. This council was to serve only "till the College is ready to commence the business of instruction"; but its effective life carried well beyond that point, for this body, together with many of its original members, was simply incorporated into the evolving structure of college governance, first as the College Council and then as the Council of Corporation.[11]

Through the deliberations and decisions of this committee we can see emerging those social, cultural, and religious doctrines that became the hallmark of Trinity College. The first of these we have already encountered. Bishop Strachan was determined to put an indelible and exclusively Anglican stamp on this new body: "As the College is to be strictly a Church of England institution, the members [of the Council] will be required to sign the Thirty Nine Articles."[12] The first meeting of the new council began with this important ritual, all those present signing the articles; those who were absent and those brought on to the council at a later date were required to sign the articles before they could assume their seats. One can also see right from the start the hierarchy of social relations that was to characterize college life. The bishop was not only the founder; he was the supreme figure in the governance of Trinity College. Although all the decisions of the council were to be decided by the majority vote of those present, Strachan had an effective veto: "No vote or resolution shall be acted upon from which the Lord Bishop shall dissent."[13]

The new council quickly approved the site Strachan had chosen and then turned to the architectural competition for the design of the building. The drawings of St Aidan's College, Birkenhead, were submitted to the competing architects, Mr Kivas Tully and Messrs Cumberland and Ridout, who were instructed "to examine that plan and give the Council such an idea of it as to enable them to determine to what extent and in what manner it would be expedient to proceed." The council also stipulated that it was prepared to expend "any sum within 8000 pounds currency ... to complete so much of the design as will enable them to open the College." It also asked each architect to give a separate estimate "for the whole design if fully carried including the Church separately estimated."[14]

Less than a month later (on 20 February 1851), the council accepted "the plans of Mr Tully" and paid £25 to the unsuccessful firm. At the same time tenders were called for the construction of the building and the painting and glazing. On 14 March the council approved the contract, which provided for "the whole of the foundations to the principal floor" and completion of "the centre building and the eastern wing." The council also accepted the lowest tender (from Metcalfe, Wilson, and Forbes); at £7,845 it was £500 less than that of its nearest competitor and the only one below the ceiling the council had imposed. The contractor hoped to cut costs by making bricks on the site, and the college agreed to meet the costs of landscaping at a later date. On St Patrick's Day, 1851, the council met at the site of the college to witness Bishop Strachan turn the first sod, in "a brief but impressive ceremony."[15]

The college building faced to the south, set back about 400 feet from Queen Street.[16] It was 250 feet in length, and, as in the plan for St Aidan's, Birkenhead, was two storeys high with three projecting bays. Short wings at both ends extended to the north for about fifty feet. The front of the building, with its symmetrical massing and Tudor detailing, clearly resembles the plan Tully had been given as a guide, and like St Aidan's, the new building was finished in brick with stone trim. The college architect departed from St Aidan's, however, in one important respect. The roofline of St Aidan's was relatively plain: there were French pavilion roofs at each end of the building, joined by a long flat roof line broken only by the peak of the central gable and four short chimneys. Kivas Tully completely reworked the design by adding three impressive towers and several other projections to the roof. Two lanterns replaced the pavilion roofs at each end of the building, one marking the provost's lodge at the southwest corner, the other the museum and library at the southeast. Then above the central gable over the main entrance, Tully placed a massive tower that dominated the entire design. Around each of these towers were smaller turrets while pinnacles rose up at the projecting angles of each bay. These were ornamented with "bosses, creepers and crockets."[17] The central ogee-domed tower, so reminiscent of the Tom Tower at Oxford, became the college landmark, and clearly it inspired the Revd Henry Scadding to muse about Trinity College as an infant Christ Church. The tower also became the dominant element of the most impressive and best remembered view of the old college: rising above the main entrance of the building, the tower terminated the view up the narrow drive from Queen

Street. The drive itself was bordered by stately trees and framed by the noble college gates, which in old photographs were always closed. The stonework of these gates, which were built in 1903, is the only part of this view that has survived.[18]

The views of the new college Tully's design constructed were suitably arresting. The east end of the building ran close to the edge of the ravine formed by the Garrison Creek – Scadding's "elmy dale"[19] – giving the college from this direction a natural appearance, if not quite the savageness that Gothic sensibilities seemed to require. This impression was further enhanced when the chapel was added to this end of the building in 1884. The view of the college from the south was also enhanced by a terrace that ran along the front of the building and extended along each side as far as the wings. The terrace fell away abruptly about ten yards in front of the building, making the design more imposing by making the building appear from a distance to be about half a storey higher than it actually was. In the original plan the terrace was to be enclosed by a stone wall, pierced by three short flights of steps, but this wall was never built.

The new college building provided for the two crucial functions that Strachan and the council were determined to combine – classroom space for academic instruction and residential accommodation for the provost and his family, the unmarried professors, and about forty-five students.[20] There were also offices for the professors (adjoining their classrooms), waiting rooms, a museum, a refectory, and "apartments for domestics." The library was to serve *pro tem* as the college chapel. The medical faculty was also to be housed in the main college building, and medical theatres were incorporated into the design for this purpose, although plans were already being considered to move the medical faculty off campus and turn this space over to more classrooms and student residences. These elements were also part of what was intended to be an even more ambitious design. The contract had called for the laying of "the whole of the foundations to the principal floor," and in this larger plan the college building was to become the south side of a full quadrangle, enclosing a space measuring 170 feet by 120 feet (with a fountain in the centre). When completed, it was to include a chapel, a museum, a dining hall, and more classrooms and professors' residences.[21] Although this plan was not followed, the arrangement it envisaged – an enclosed medieval quadrangle set beside a wooded ravine just beyond the reach of the city – captured the residential and isolated elements that were central to the founders' educational philosophy.

Although the champions of the college were anxious to praise the beauty of the building and invest it with a host of religious, historical, and romantic associations, it should be pointed out that the actual construction of Trinity College was in many ways an object lesson in poor craftsmanship and a litany of things gone wrong. Two elements specified in the contract – the laying of the foundations for the whole quadrangle and the construction of the east wing – were not carried out. And what was completed at this time proved to be medieval in a way the council had clearly not intended. On 9 March 1852 the architect was called to appear before the council and "informed of the bad state of the building in several places"; when it rained the turrets leaked, when the fireplaces were lit the rooms filled with smoke, and when the council inspected the provost's lodge, Kivas Tully was summoned once again to explain why he had failed to provide the Provost and his family with bedrooms, a "bath room," and a "water closet."[22]

The building of such an elaborate structure was also enormously expensive; and paying for it was both a trial in itself and a form of initiation into a mode of crisis management that would characterize the early financial history of the college. The college had paid £2000 for the site, with the cost of the building and the preparation of the grounds, costs rose quickly to over £13,000, and the architect and contractor came before council regularly to ask for more money.[23] Annual expenditures were also considerable. Professorial salaries were £1,200, and added to this were administrative costs (for a bursar and book-keeper) and house expenditures (for maintenance and servants), as well as taxes, insurance, and incidental expenses. According to the college accounts in 1858, these annual expenditures amounted to well over £4,000.[24] The Diocesan Theological Institute in Cobourg, it is important to point out, had chosen to follow a very different financial path. It had been started on a shoestring, and as it grew, it had always kept well within its allotted resources. At its height the Institute managed to get on quite well, supported entirely by an annual charge of £1,200 on the clergy reserves. This covered Bethune's stipend and a small allowance towards his housing, paid the salary of a tutor, and allowed for £300 to £400 a year for scholarships. In marked contrast, the construction of Trinity College was an enormous undertaking, and the expense of building, maintaining, and runing the college quickly stretched the resources of the college to their very limits.

Many of the problems the college encountered in trying to meet these costs can be traced at least in the first instance to the new financial circumstances into which the college had been born. The transition from state church to private denomination had placed the raising of money on an entirely new footing. King's College had been richly endowed by the state with vast amounts of crown lands; and the new University of Toronto not only inherited this endowment, which in 1855 was valued at $1,175,000 and yielded about $60,000 annually, but as the provincial university it could also try to appeal to the state as the need arose.[25] Trinity had none of these revenues. Right from the start it was clear that the college was "to be endowed from private sources only," and on 29 May

1850 Strachan set down a plan for raising the necessary funds. He calculated that £25,000 to £30,000 could be raised in the colony, and this money would then be "expended in erecting the necessary buildings." He would then turn to Britain in order to raise an endowment for the operating expenses of the college. Here he hoped to draw on two sources. He wanted to appeal directly to the British public by having a letter from the Queen read in all the churches, which he anticipated would bring in about £20,000. He also hoped to raise a further £10,000 by appealing on his own to "public bodies and individuals in England."[26]

As Strachan prepared to advance upon his British prey, the Church University Board (the General Board to Promote the Interests of the Church University) proceeded quickly with the provincial part of this strategy. On 7 February 1850, shortly before he left for Britain, Strachan wrote a pastoral letter to the clergy and laity that repeated the now familiar history of the secularization of King's College and called on the members of the church to support the proposed university.[27] Two highly respected clergy, the Revds T.B. Fuller and Saltern Givens, were then placed in charge of the canvass, and they proceeded to circulate subscription lists through every parish in the Diocese of Toronto.[28] As was the custom these lists were headed up by the names of prominent people who had set a good example by pledging large sums to the cause. They included Alexander Burnside, Enoch Turner, Andrew Mercer, Justice Draper, Vice-Chancellor Jamieson, the Bishop of Toronto, and the Revds Herchmer and Stennett.[29]

The results of this provincial canvass must have been enormously gratifying, especially given the problems of raising capital of any kind in the colonial economy. The first financial statement of the college – "a financial abstract of the disposable resources and endowment of Trinity College" – was presented to the Provisional Council on 6 November 1851. It calculated that about

£26,000 had been raised in the Diocese of Toronto. This included about £5,000 in money, £4,500 in building stock, £10,000 in land, and £7,000 left by will. The SPG had also turned over to the college a parcel of town lots, valued at £5,000 that it had purchased on the Garrison Reserve. These benefactions were recorded in the minutes of the council, and in keeping with a policy established at the second meeting of the Church University Board on 18 April 1850, were placed in a separate and supposedly permanent list, and then published and circulated.[30]

Though these early lists are far from complete, they are nonetheless very revealing. They are headed by the "special donors," whose pledges, much of it in land, came to £8,500. Less well acknowledged, however, was the broad base of financial support within the church that the college enjoyed. Subscriptions came in from about fifty-seven parishes and totalled about £17,000 – close to two-thirds of the amount raised. These parishes were spread throughout the Diocese of Toronto, although the contributions tended to be concentrated in parishes between Cobourg in the east and Woodstock in the west, with parishes in Toronto, Hamilton, and the Niagara Peninsula especially strongly represented. No contribution, it is interesting to note, was recorded from the parish of St Paul's, London, Canada West, the parish of the Revd Benjamin Cronyn and the See city of what became the Diocese of Huron in 1857. Altogether 450 persons contributed to the college, many of them subscribing amounts under £10, either in money or building stock.[31] All this was done in great haste; if there had been more time, Strachan asserted, the number of contributors and total contributed would have been even higher.

In Britain, however, the appeal for funds was almost a complete failure. Bishop Strachan was not granted a letter from the Queen, and his second line of appeal – to public bodies and individuals –

also fell far short of the mark. He had hoped to raise £30,000 in Britain; he returned to Canada with pledges for only £10,000. Archdeacon Bethune also tried to raise funds for the college when he was in Britain the following year,[32] only to encounter similar difficulties. Although received warmly, he was able to add only £800 to what the bishop had raised.[33] Another disturbing sign for the future health of the college can also be gleaned from the names of those who did come forward at this time. Most of the money raised in these British appeals came from the two great church societies. While their donations were at once generous and welcome, both of these bodies had already made it clear that they intended to end their donations to Toronto in order to support the church in other, and much needier, parts of the empire. The SPG nonetheless voted Trinity a special grant of £2,000 and turned over to the college the lands it had purchased on the Garrison Common. And then in 1852, to commemorate the one hundred and fiftieth anniversary of the founding of the Society, the SPG gave the college another £1,000 to fund the Jubilee scholarships.[34] The other great missionary society, the Society for Promoting Christian Knowledge, was also very generous, giving £3,000 to the college. Oxford University also gave Trinity £500.[35]

Faced with such a shortfall, the Bishop searched desperately for new sources of support.[36] The Revd William McMurray was given testimonial letters (and an honorary degree) and then dispatched on a fundraising trip to the United States – an interesting enterprise given Strachan's long-standing criticisms of American society in general and American universities in particular. McMurray was, nonetheless, extraordinarily successful; over the next two years he visited the United States three times and raised more than $10,000 in books and money.[37] His obvious talents as a fundraiser made him an invaluable agent of the college, and a few years later he was dispatched on an expedition to Britain, where he was able to solicit donations from both Gladstone and Pusey. A portrait of this important but little-known figure hangs in Seeley Hall.[38]

Given the precarious state of the college's finances, Strachan's next step was to be crucial to the life of the college. He was determined to turn the revenue that was coming to the church from the clergy reserves to the advantage of the new church university. As a first step he made sure that the annual grant of £1,200 from the clergy reserve surplus fund, which he and the SPG had designated for theological education at Cobourg, was now transferred to Trinity College. Without this revenue from the old state-church system, which Strachan accepted without hesitation, one doubts if Trinity would been able to open its doors. Three years later, when the revenue from the clergy reserves was secularized, Strachan made every effort to have Trinity College share in the commutation scheme. "If the Clergy Reserve Bill cannot be arrested," he instructed the Revd Ernest Hawkins, the Secretary of the SPG, "endeavour to get the present charges made perpetual and not confined to the lives of the Incumbents. Especially make the charge of 1,200 pounds for the support of Trinity College permanent, otherwise in a few years it will be put in extreme difficulty."[39] This scheme, however, was only partially successful. The commutation clauses protected only the financial interests of the clergy who were receiving support from the reserves; once they died the payments would cease. But the bishop made the most of a bad situation. Working closely with John Hillyard Cameron (a future chancellor) he tried to have Trinity as an institution included in the commutation scheme. When this too failed, he lobbied successfully to have all three Trinity professors, who were ordained clergymen, placed on the commutation lists.[40] Since the amount each received from the commutation fund was based upon life expectancy, their youth proved to be a singular financial asset. The combined total of the their commutation came to £16,465/4[41] – which was then cleverly separated from the general commutation fund and paid directly to Trinity College, where it once again saved the fledgling institution from financial ruin.[42]

There is an aura of quiet but understandable desperation in all this searching for money. After all, trying to finance a church college from private sources alone was something new for the church, and no one was at all certain if it could be done. In many ways the founders responded very creatively to this new situation: they canvassed their own members effectively, carried their appeal to both Britain and the United States, and (in the case of the clergy reserves) managed to pull a sizable rabbit out of an old top hat. At the same time, however, financing an institution is not just a matter of collecting, and then spending, money. Financial goals and strategies – how money should be raised, who should be approached, and the ways in which money should be spent – are based on important social and cultural attitudes that can deeply influence the life and well-being of an institution. Here one can discern in the initial steps to finance Trinity College the persistence of a number of older assumptions about church finance that were to have a long-term influence on the financial health of the college.

To finance itself in the past, the church had relied on a combination of subscriptions, endowments, and fees. When a parish was to be built up, the local community would be called upon to donate money and labour to build (or rebuild) the local church and rectory. As a rule this campaign would be carried out by the local clergyman and a few prominent members of the parish, who would canvass for subscriptions. It was essential, however, that the next major item of expenditure, the stipend of the clergyman, be kept quite separate from this initial appeal. In keeping with establishment thinking, the clergyman was a gentleman who should not have to depend for his stipend upon the financial goodwill of those he ministered to. For this reason clerical salaries were supported from endowed sources that were independent of congregational control. In Canada this meant that stipends should be funded either directly or indirectly by the state – from the casual and territorial revenue of the crown, through the SPG, which received government grants, and also from the revenue raised from the clergy reserves. Finally, money was needed for the ongoing administrative costs of the parish, which usually meant keeping the church and the church yard in reasonable repair. For this the church relied upon the annual fees paid by the pew holders for their pews. There were also fees paid for particular services, such as marriages and burials, which could support the upkeep of the church, although one imagines most of these went directly into the rector's pocket.

In a curious way many of these older assumptions about raising and spending money carried over into the financing of Trinity College. The actual costs of building the college were treated like those of a parish church in that money was subscribed by a local canvass and then devoted almost entirely to the acquisition of the site and the construction of the college building. The salaries of the professors were to be looked after in much the same way as clerical salaries had been dealt with in the old system, that is, from endowed sources. In this case the endowment came from the money raised in Britain, to which was added the grant for theological education from the clergy reserves and then the large lump sum the college received from the commutation fund, as well as the money from the sale of the SPG property on the Garrison Reserve. This then left the day-to-day costs of the college, which, in effect, were to be covered by the academic equivalent of pew rents – the fees students paid for their terms and whatever other fees the college was able to charge.

These older cultural assumptions about raising and spending

money were to have serious consequences for the college's finances. But at the moment everyone was caught up in the rush to open the college as quickly as possible. The most pressing financial question was to find enough money for the immediate expenditures, and in this situation the finance committee presented the Provisional Council with the first, bare-bones college budget – the estimates of expenditures and revenues for the college "to go into operation." Annual expenditures were £1,716 (made up of professorial salaries and "contingencies"), while revenues totalled £1,150. These were made up of £900 from the SPG (the annual grant of £1,200 less £300 set aside for scholarships) and £250 from fees. The difference of about £550 between expenditure and revenue was to be made up by drawing on the capital in the endowment.[43] Looking ahead, one can see this pattern of deficits starting to become ingrained. In 1859, for example, a more detailed statement of the college accounts shows both the state of the endowment and the annual revenues and expenditures. After deducting the expenses of buildings, grounds, furniture, museum, and taxes (about £16,000) from the total amount raised from all sources (about £70,500),[44] the college was left with an endowment of about £54,000. The college's annual operating revenue was then derived from the interest on this endowment, which in that year yielded £2,200, and the "Fees from Students," which yielded £1,500. Total revenue for the year was then £3,701. On the expenditure side the two largest items were the salaries of the professors and staff (about £1,800) and house expenditures (£1,788); with the addition of a number of small items the total expenditure came to £4,186. In this year expenditures exceeded income by £485, which was made up once again by drawing on the capital in the endowment.[45]

It did not take a degree in divinity to prophesy where such financial practices, if left unchecked, would lead. Drawing upon the endowment to meet annual deficits lowered the value of the endowment and reduced the amount of revenue the endowment produced, and would in time lead to the collapse of both the endowment and its contribution to the annual income. Such an end, however, was by no means imminent, and before its arrival the college could continue to look for more benefactions. There was also the hope, once the college had opened successfully, of increased enrolments and a nice rise in fee income. There was enough money in the bank and sincerely pledged for the college to go forward. Indeed, acquiring new donors and students largely depended upon the college's opening as quickly as possible. So amid this financial uncertainty, Strachan and the Provisional Council took up the task of acquiring the professors who would teach and oversee the collegiate life of the new college.

Strachan turned to England and his old and trusted ally, the Revd Ernest Hawkins, the secretary of the Society for the Propagation of the Gospel. He was determined to find men with high academic credentials, and no clergy serving in Canada were even considered, even though many of them had decent university degrees.[46] Hawkins set up a Trinity College Committee in London. It was composed of four very prominent clergymen: in addition to Hawkins, who kept Strachan informed of the committee's progress, there was the Revd John Jackson, rector of St James and later Lord Bishop of London; the Revd Charles B. Dalton, rector of Lambeth and chaplain to the bishop of London; and the Revd Henry McKenzie, vicar of St Martin-in-the-Fields and later suffragan bishop of Nottingham. McKenzie also served as treasurer of the committee, a task that included receiving the subscriptions that Strachan and Bethune had solicited in their recent fund-raising campaigns in England.[47]

In a long letter written to the committee on 16 February 1851, Strachan described the type of men he wanted and the duties they would be called upon to perform. "The College," he wrote rather grandiloquently, "is intended to supply a fit education for the youth of Canada containing more than a million of Inhabitants speaking the English language."[48] Teaching in the college was to be organized under three heads – the theological, the classical, and the scientific – with a faculty member assigned to each area: "the Provost or Head and two professors." He then turned to the issue at hand. "My present object therefore in writing is to request you to select three gentlemen willing to devote themselves for some years or longer as they please to the founding and raising up of a University worthy of the name." Here Strachan introduced a metaphor that he would return to time and again as he described the character of the new college. These three men were to be entrusted with "building up the Institution ... as it respects the instruction, discipline, and the economical management on the principle of the whole constituting one large family." In effect, it was the provost and the new professors who would be called upon, while walking this taut financial tightrope, to transform the framework that the bishop and the council had set up into a collegiate family, "a University worthy of the name."

In keeping with the religious tests he had imposed on the members of the Provisional Council, Strachan insisted not only that all the faculty be members of the church, but also that the provost (and if possible all the professors) be priests. It is instructive to note that this requirement was linked to the residential, rather than the strictly religious, life of the college. The college was to be run as a well-ordered, highly regulated family, and Strachan wanted the type of men who could carry out their duty in overseeing such a family without flinching, "for we think that clergymen find it more easy to keep up strict Collegiate discipline and internal arrangements." Strachan was also well aware of the fierce battles being fought in England over Tractarianism, as well

as the growing party divisions in his own diocese. For this reason
he added specific injunctions about the position these men should
occupy within the church: "We are anxious that the three belong
to neither extreme of the Church but that they should be true
Sons of the Church of England as you all are – not low or what
is called Evangelical but well imbued with her distinctive principles and equally distant from Romanism on the one hand and
dissent on the other." Once again time was of the essence. Strachan wanted all three men to be in Toronto by mid-September,
for the council intended to begin instruction by 1 October. Anticipating the difficulties the committee might encounter in per-
suading suitable candidates to come out to the colonies, the
bishop closed his letter by holding out what he believed to be the
most compelling inducement of the appointment: "It is seldom
that an opportunity of doing good on so large a scale is offered
to young men entering life."[49] Over fifty years before, the young
John Strachan had been drawn to Upper Canada by the promise
of just such an opportunity.

The committee did indeed encounter difficulties in filling these
positions; at least one clergyman (after some hesitation) declined
the provostship, and another who had apparently accepted the
position in mathematics had to be replaced at the last moment.[50]
Nevertheless, the three men the committee selected to constitute
the professoriate of the new colonial university satisfied Strachan's
requirements very well. The professor of classics was the Revd
Edward St John Parry, MA, aged 26 and a graduate of Balliol College, Oxford; and the professor of mathematics was the Revd
George Clerk Irving, MA, aged 23, from St John's College, Cambridge. The provost and professor of divinity was the Revd
George Whitaker, MA, from Queen's College, Cambridge, where
he had been a foundation fellow and taught classics. At the time
he was approached by the committee, Whitaker had been the

vicar of Oakington, a parish in Cambridgeshire, for ten years. He was married, had a substantial family, and had just turned forty. Taken together, the three men were very well educated, were startlingly young, and were all in holy orders. The bishop seemed very pleased indeed, and once again we can listen to the founder's sense of satisfaction as he effortlessly runs together academic qualifications and considerations of social class. "We are very fortunate," he confided to the bishop of Nova Scotia, "in the three professors whom we procured from England two from Cambridge and one from Oxford. They are not only first rate men as Scholars but of very gentlemanly bearing and courteous manners."[51]

The Revd George Whitaker, who was inducted as provost of Trinity College by Bishop Strachan on 8 December 1851, was to have an especially formative influence on Trinity College.[52] As the first provost he created the curriculum and devised many of the initial rules and regulations, and he was able to cultivate and secure his handiwork over a period of thirty years, a term that none of his successors has even approached. During his entire career he was also the professor of divinity, in which capacity he taught every student in arts and divinity. In effect, it was wellnigh impossible to pass through Trinity without escaping the solemn gaze of the great G. Whitaker.

Whitaker was born on 9 October 1811 in Bratton, Wiltshire. He grew up in a large, close-knit, and deeply religious family that encouraged reading, education, and literary attainments. He was the eighth of the nine children of Philip and Anne Whitaker. The Whitakers were not Anglican, but were devout Baptists, leading members of the Bratton chapel, where George's father was a lay reader. His mother was the daughter of a dissenting minister. The family had been farmers for generations. Philip Whitaker raised sheep on a tract of more than 900 acres that he leased from a member of the local gentry, Richard Erle Drax Grosvenor. He also owned a freehold of some seventy-six acres in the Manor of Bratton.[53] The Whitakers were respectable people; Philip was an important man in the village and in this part of the county. Although he would not have been counted among the gentry, he was considerably more than a tenant; he had the substance to be his own man if not quite all the official attributes of gentility.

After attending Frome Grammar School, young George was sent to Charterhouse School in London, where he enrolled as a day boy, living with his older brother Edward, who had established himself as a solicitor in London a few years before. From Charterhouse he went up to Queen's College, Cambridge, in 1829. Three years later he was baptized at Bratton Parish Church and became a member of the Church of England. This took place two days after he had turned twenty-one and at the beginning of the academic year in which he was required to subscribe to the Articles of Religion in order to take his degree. In the parish register he described himself as a gentleman, a position he had earned rather than inherited. The year after taking his degree he was offered a foundation fellowship by his college. According to the custom of the university, fellows were required to be in holy orders, and George was duly ordered deacon at age twenty-five and ordained a year later. In his college he lectured in classics. Then in 1840 he left Cambridge, accepted a living that was in the gift of his college, and moved into the substantial Georgian vicarage of Oakington. By giving up his fellowship he was also at liberty to take a wife, and in 1844 he married Arundel Charlotte Burton. Together they would have at least eight children.

There are several points of correspondence between Whitaker's life in England and the way he would shape Trinity College. The strong religious convictions he brought to his new position were firmly instilled by his family, and although he was not Anglican by birth, his transition to the Church of England (which his family supported) seems to have only strengthened his religious resolve. In fact, neither of the other two founders of Trinity College was Anglican by birth. Both John Strachan and Alexander Bethune had previously belonged to other Protestant churches, however much the former tried to conceal the fact.

The Cambridge that Whitaker attended in the 1830s – clerical and unreformed – clearly served as a model for many things at Trinity. The new college curriculum of divinity, classics, and mathematics was based on that of Cambridge and changed very little during Whitaker's time in office. Many of the oaths of office Whitaker introduced were literally transcribed from those at Cambridge and other British universities.[54] All the while, however, a deeper current from Whitaker's early career runs through the first three decades of the history of Trinity College. His progress in life seemed to confirm the efficacy of the new exclusively Anglican vision that Bishop Strachan held out for the college and the colonial church. As we have seen, Trinity was securely tied to the church and also tried to draw an alliance of church grammar schools into its orbit; the schools would lead students into Trinity where they would be prepared for a career as teachers, clergy, and the other learned professions. George Whitaker's undoubted talents had been nurtured and rewarded by his advancement through precisely this kind of Anglican *cursus honorum*. As a young boy he had entered one of the great schools of England, and being a Carthusian undoubtedly helped to prepare his way into Cambridge. After completing his undergraduate career successfully, Whitaker was drawn further into this clerical-academic structure by becoming a member of the Church of England in order to take his degree and then by accepting ordination in order to take up his foundation fellowship to teach in his college. He then moved from the life of a scholar to the life of a parish clergyman by exchanging, as it were, a college fellowship for a college living. This career

path was interrupted for thirty years by the call from the Trinity
Committee in London to take up the provostship of Trinity College, Toronto. Once at Toronto he proceeded as if by instinct to
try to fashion the same clerical-academic system that had served
him so well in Britain. In effect, he took the structure set up by
Strachan and the council and proceeded to shape it in a way that
was thoroughly consistent with their goals, but that also reflected
Whitaker's own attitudes, beliefs, and experiences.

The legislation incorporating Trinity College was introduced
into the provincial legislature in May 1851 and passed later in the
same session. Although much ado was made at that time and in
the future about the critical role of the Royal Charter the college
received on 16 July 1852, this provincial legislation provided the
legal bedrock for the new college, a point well understood by the
College Council.[55] But Strachan had fought hard for a Royal
Charter, and it quickly acquired great symbolic significance.
Unfortunately, it came to be seen as the necessary founding document and something that superseded the provincial legislation
rather than something that was appended to it.[56]

Acting under the provisions of the provincial legislation, Strachan now appointed all the men who were serving on the Provisional Council to the new "Council of Trinity College," which
met for the first time on 17 September 1851. On 6 November it
was announced that Whitaker and Parry had arrived and on 13
November that the building would be ready to receive the first
students by 16 January 1852. The council now turned to the difficult task of framing statutes and regulations for the college; a
committee consisting of Strachan, the Provost, the two professors
and the Revd H.J. Grasett was appointed "to draft the rules and
regulations for the internal government of the College and the
statutes thereof." On 27 November "Professor Parry read the

statutes which the committee appointed to draft rules and regulations" had drawn up. Following the procedures set down by council, notice was given that these would be considered at the next meeting, and on 4 December, with all the professors present the first eleven statutes of Trinity College were "ordained and enacted" under the authority of the Provincial Act of Incorporation.[57] Dealing primarily with matters of position and authority, they expanded upon many of the college's social and religious doctrines. The religious tests imposed on the provost and the faculty were now enforced by statute. Other statutes defined the power of the bishop (or future bishops) to appoint and remove professors (cause must be stated in writing), ranked the professors in relation to other members of council, and specified their salaries. The ninth statute – "the duties of the provost and of the several Professors shall be such as shall from time to time be declared by the Statutes, Orders, and Regulations of the College Council" – appeared on the surface to provide a way for the rules of the college to evolve as the need arose.[58]

The controversy, however, that flared up around the wording of this statute reveals a good deal about both the hierarchy within the governing structure and the future character of college life. On 9 December 1851, the day after he had become provost, Whitaker wrote a letter (co-signed by Parry and Irving) objecting to the ninth article. They argued that the article was too loose and might lead to interference by the council in the day-to-day life of the college. To regulate college life, they asserted, the provost and the professors must have the power to define and control the details of their own work. Whitaker invoked the metaphor Strachan had used in his letter to the committee in London. If the domestic life of the college was to be constructed on "the principle that the institution constituted one large family," then surely, he argued, just as children are responsible to their parents, so the students and servants should be responsible to "their ordinary superiors" and not the more distant College Council.[59]

Although the statute in question remained intact, additional statutes were adopted that effectively gave Whitaker everything he wanted, by placing the provost and the professors in charge of the students, the servants, and all the academic and disciplinary arrangements of the college.[60] This controversy also clarified the social and religious hierarchy that was central to the structure of the college. Strachan, as bishop and founder, was still acknowledged as the highest-ranking person in the college. At the same time the new statutes shielded the provost and established his authority over the internal affairs of college life. Although immediately below the bishop, he now had his own distinct sphere of authority, namely, all things pertaining to the academic and social life of the college. Whitaker had also accomplished something few others had managed to do during Strachan's long episcopate: he had challenged the bishop's authority and managed to remain on good terms with him.

Once this issue was out of the way the council quickly agreed to a series of detailed "Regulations for Students in Arts" and "Regulations for Theological Students." Again a set of now familiar social and cultural assumptions was codified into a body of domestic law. It almost goes without saying that religious (and other kinds of) tests figured very prominently in this exercise. All students who entered Trinity College were required to declare upon matriculation that they would obey the laws of the college and "diligently attend to the studies required." But students entering divinity also had to sign the articles of religion, and at graduation every student in every faculty had to sign the following declaration: "I, A.B., do willingly and heartily declare that I am truly and sincerely a member of the United Church of England

and Ireland." In effect, though students in arts and medicine did not have to be Anglican to enter Trinity College, they had to be a member of the church in order to leave with a degree. This recalls the course followed by Whitaker, who had joined the established church in his graduation year in order to take his degree from Cambridge. And, once again this highly restrictive religious test was not hidden under a bushel, but published almost defiantly in the college calendar.[61]

The same body of regulations also reinforced the strong religious character of college life. That religious services in the college chapel were to be conducted according to the rites and practices of the United Church of England and Ireland goes without saying; the statutes, however, went a good deal further in stipulating that chapel services were to be frequent and compulsory. Morning and Evening Prayer were read each day, and "every person resident in College shall attend at such services." There were also special services on Sundays and saints' days. Indeed one can almost smell the strong monastic air that hung over these rules: not only were these religious services to bring the community together at certain appointed hours, but they were also essentially private affairs, closed to members of the outside world. By statute, "strangers" who wanted to worship in the chapel on Sundays and other special occasions were required to "apply for permission to the Provost."[62]

The founders' final task was in many ways the most important. If Trinity College was to become a "university worthy of the name," it had to have a strong and impressive curriculum. Under the skilful direction of Provost Whitaker, the council now set about creating that web of courses and regulations that would enclose the academic lives of the students from the moment they applied for entry to the time they took their degrees. The curriculum was very self-consciously a public document; it was first published as part of the official statutes and regulations of the college and then reprinted annually in the college calendars. In constructing the curriculum Whitaker drew heavily upon his own academic experience as a student and teaching fellow at Cambridge.[63] He divided the courses of instruction into three broad areas of study, divinity, classics, and mathematics. The last of these encompassed topics such as statics, dynamics, and optics that would now be considered a part of science.[64] Students in arts studied all these subjects for three years, whereas students in the theological course concentrated almost exclusively on divinity for another two years of study. The academic year was divided into three terms: Michaelmas (from 1 October to 20 December), Lent (from 10 January to the second Saturday before Easter), and Easter (from the Saturday after Easter to 1 July).[65]

To take a bachelor's degree in arts, students were required to "keep" (that is, enrol for) nine terms and pass three sets of college examinations. The first was the formal matriculation examination, which students wrote as they entered the college. Here the students (who had to be at least fifteen years of age) were examined in scripture history and the Greek Testament, Latin and Greek authors, and mathematics (arithmetic, algebra, and simple geometry). This examination, which was marked "with particular attention ... paid to grammatical accuracy,"[66] was designed to reassure the college that matriculating students arrived with an elementary knowledge of the three general areas of study they would pursue over the next three years. It was assumed that students who had attended a good grammar school would be able to pass this test with little difficulty, and in 1878 the college allowed prospective students to forgo the matriculation examination if they presented "a certificate from the proper authorities that [they had] passed satisfactorily the intermediate examination of High Schools and Collegiate Institutes."[67] The second examination, which was called the "previous examination," took place at the end of the Lent term in the second year, in effect about halfway through the three-year course of study. At this point all the students in arts were examined on a historical book of the New Testament, Paley's *Evidences of Christianity*, the Church Catechism, a Latin and a Greek author, Latin prose, algebra, trigonometry, and Euclid. The third examination, the "examination for the Degree of Bachelor of Arts" (popularly called the "final" examination), consisted of Old and New Testament history, another historical book of the New Testament, two Greek and two Latin authors, Greek and Roman history, Latin composition, geometry, algebra, trigonometry, mechanics, and hydrostatics.[68] To achieve honours standing, students then wrote a separate set of examinations, usually after the final examination. Rather than being tied to specific courses, the college examinations examined the students on a predetermined list of texts, which was published in the college calendar every year, together with the names of the students who had achieved honours standing in the examinations the previous year.[69]

The three-year programme in arts and the bachelor's degree provided in turn the foundation for what was officially called "the Theological course of study." Indeed in their initial formulation the regulations specified that having a BA from Trinity College was the *only* way one could enter the theological course. During this two-year programme students studied only divinity, perhaps explaining the popular (but misleading) practice of using the term "Divinity" to distinguish the theological programme from the programme in arts. Candidates preparing for ordination were to receive instruction in the Holy Scriptures in their original languages, the Thirty-nine Articles of Religion, the *Book of Common Prayer*, church history, and "such Ethical subjects as are now closely connected with Theology." The initial college regulations also expressed the hope that "arrangements will be made for giving the Theology Students some practical acquaintance with parochial duties," although no specific programme was established for this purpose.[70] After completing the theological course (keeping six terms in divinity), candidates were considered ready to leave the college and, if they had attained the proper canonical age, to present themselves for ordination.

But before long, the requirement that the study of theology be preceded by three years in the arts programme was abandoned. The pressing need for clergy and the high financial cost of a five-year sojourn at Trinity compelled the authorities to find ways of moving these students through the college more quickly. Consequently, students going into divinity were allowed to begin the theological course while still undergraduates in arts. Upon application to the provost, students who had attained the age of twenty-one could enter divinity after they had completed only one year in the arts course.[71] Although it is impossible to know exactly how many students availed themselves of this provision, there is no doubt that this shortened route – a year or two in arts followed by two years in divinity – became a very well-travelled path.

In 1865 the college further revised the initial design by accepting mature men into the theological course who did not have any undergraduate training whatsoever, provided they offered suitable testimonials, passed an entrance examination that was similar to the divinity sections of the matriculation examination, and then completed "without fail" the two years of the theological course. This innovation was in fact very similar to the one made in 1860 for mature men entering arts, but then discontinued in 1864.[72] At the same time the college tried to enlarge its intake of theological students by allowing students to enter divinity who had received their BAs from church universities other than Trinity College, namely, Oxford, Cambridge, Trinity College Dublin, Durham,

King's (Windsor), King's (Fredericton), Bishop's (Lennoxville), and "the late King's College, Toronto."[73]

All these changes point to a basic flaw in the original design of the college curriculum. Such a demanding entrance requirement into the theological course (a three-year BA from Trinity College) severely limited the number of students who could qualify and reduced the number of clergy the college was able to present to the church for ordination. These new provisions for entering and leaving the programme were intended to bring more candidates into divinity and allow those who were in the college to move through their preparation more quickly. At the same time, the college took steps to protect its broader academic and social goals. First, both of these shortened paths to ordination were closely guarded by substantial social and academic regulations. Students with one or two years in arts who wished to enter divinity before completing their BA had to be twenty-one years of age and receive permission from the provost, and given the small size of the college and the structure of the curriculum, the provost would have known each applicant personally. Mature men who came from outside the college and entered divinity directly had to "obtain the recommendation of the Clergyman of their parish, countersigned by a Bishop," and then pass an entrance examination and complete "without exception" the full two-year course in divinity.[74]

The second set of precautions was more informal. These new dispensations clearly threatened one of the prime social and theological goals of Trinity College: to create clergy who had both theological training and a bachelor's degree. Consequently, the college went to enormous lengths to encourage those who had entered divinity without a BA to acquire it before they left the college. "A man of diligence and fair ability,"[75] the provost pointed out, who entered divinity from arts before completing his BA could continue his undergraduate work while studying theology and, by sitting successfully the previous and final examinations and adding the six terms of the divinity course to the three he had completed in arts, could satisfy all the degree requirements. In effect, candidates could study arts and divinity concurrently, and complete both in three or four years instead of five. The way to the BA for mature students entering divinity by testimonials and examination was more difficult, but if they remained at the college for one more year (and thereby kept the full nine terms) and wrote both the previous and final examinations, they too would be eligible to apply for their bachelor's degree. It is interesting to note that many mature students who had gone directly into divinity and then been ordained without a BA were kept on the college books as undergraduates long after they had left the college, some remaining in this pending category for over twenty years. In effect, the college continued to hold out hope that these men would still return to Trinity at some future date to complete their degrees, a fact that indicates just how strongly Trinity held on to the notion that all the clergy it produced must have a university degree.[76]

Certainly one of the most striking features of the college curriculum as a whole is the pride of place given to the study of religion and doctrine throughout the academic programme. Trinity College had been founded, we have been told repeatedly, because the founders believed that religion must not be separated from higher education. Here we can see how the curriculum gave effect to this great college commandment. As one would expect, the careful study of the scriptures, the creeds, and the doctrines and history of the church constituted almost the entire field of scholarly endeavour for students in the theological course. But the study of religion was by no means the exclusive preserve of candidates who were preparing for ordination. Religion and doctrine permeated the arts programme in three ways. First of all, during this period the teaching of classics and mathematics, the other two core subjects in the college curriculum, was entrusted to men who were clerks in holy orders. In this way the college could be assured that instruction in what might be considered secular subjects would take place in a safe religious environment regulated by the proper moral tone.

Secondly, students in arts were required in their final year to attend, and were then examined upon, a special course of lectures in "physiology in its relation to natural theology."[77] This course was offered by Dr James Bovell, a founding member of the Faculty of Medicine, and after the resignation of that faculty in 1857, the professor of physiology in Trinity College.[78] In this rich and wide-ranging course Dr Bovell examined the structure and organization of the natural world and then drew two important precepts from his observations and the commentaries of other scientists: that there was order and design in nature and that these facts not only proved the existence of God but also demonstrated our moral duties to both the creator and his creation.[79] In his own words, these lectures were "undertaken with a view to induce the Canadian Student to engage in the study of natural science, and to contemplate the works of creation, with the object of deducing therefrom principles calculated to improve the mind, and to furnish the moral nature with such food for reflection as may elevate and adorn, rather than degrade and corrupt it."[80] Dr Bovell's course drew the study of the material world together and explained how science, when properly conducted, reinforced the story set down in the Bible, and like the Bible, gave us clear instructions on how to lead a moral life. Placed at the end of the three-year programme in arts, this course served both intellectually and structurally as a capstone to the scientific parts of the college curriculum.

This particular feature of the college's academic programme, however, was by no means unique. As Brian McKillop has pointed out, in requiring all students to take a course in natural theology, and then placing the course at such a pivotal point in the academic programme, Trinity was conforming to the practice of almost all Anglo-Canadian universities during the Victorian period.[81] What set Trinity apart from most other Anglo-Canadian universities, however, was the third way in which religion permeated the college curriculum. At Trinity, students in arts were also required in each year to take a course in divinity that placed the study of the Bible and "the outlines of Ecclesiastical History"[82] firmly within the doctrines and practices of a specific church. In effect, students in arts not only studied the way in which the Bible and nature confirmed the existence of God and the righteousness of God's commandments, they also received (from the provost) instruction in the doctrines and formularies of the United Church of England and Ireland, which Whitaker's pedagogical methods made sure they would commit to memory.

Infusing the curriculum with religion in this way also served a more practical purpose. By requiring all students to study divinity in every year of the undergraduate programme, the college was able to use the arts course not only to lead students to the bachelor's degree, but also to prepare students for the theological course of study. For students in arts the study of divinity was an end in itself; they would leave the college with a broad knowledge of the Bible, church history, and doctrine, and such knowledge would make them well-informed members of the laity. For students intending to go on to ordination, these undergraduate courses in divinity also provided a good grounding in the subjects they would study in the theological programme. For this reason the study of divinity was organized into two stages: the "elementary elements" of divinity were taught as part of the programme in arts so that students going on to the theological course would be prepared for the "higher parts of Divinity."[83] This practice of using arts as a pre-divinity programme is also confirmed by the practice of treating a number of arts students as pre-divinity students completing one or two years in arts before obtaining permission to enter the theological course of study.

Religion and doctrine bound the curriculum together and reinforced the character of Trinity College as a distinctively Church university. Speaking at the installation of John Beverley Robinson, the first chancellor of the college, Bishop Strachan alluded to the two great books "from which all knowledge and wisdom must be drawn."[84] First he named "the Book of Revelation." This book contained the Holy Scriptures, the very words of God; it was unchanging, infinite, and eternal. He then turned to "the Book of Nature." This book contained all the works of God and was "mortal, finite, and the child of time."[85] The curriculum of Trinity College, in effect, was structured in such a way that every undergraduate, whether destined for the church or the world, would learn as a good Anglican not only how to read these two great texts but also how to draw from them the single set of moral lessons that both the word of God and the gifts of God were intended to convey.

––––––

These then were the founding doctrines of Trinity College, the social, intellectual, and cultural assumptions that were poured into the vessel created by the Bishop of Toronto. Trinity was a church college constructed at a private site. It was residential and set apart from the world outside. The campus was not only built beyond the temptations of the city; it was protected by a fence, and bars were placed on the lower windows so that all the comings out and the goings in could be monitored and controlled. Inside these walls was an exclusively Anglican and carefully ordered male community of scholars, governed in all its parts by a seemingly monastic rule strictly enforced by professors in holy orders. The doctrines and formularies of the United Church of England and Ireland informed both the academic and the residential life of the institution, for all students were required to study divinity and to attend services of worship. The same spirit also regulated the social life of the institution. The days were ordered not only by the academic programme and the compulsory religious services but also by the formality of meals and the strict code for dressing. Students were required to put on the cap and gown in chapel, in hall, and at lectures, and, as if to strike terror into the hearts of the world beyond the gates, they also had to wear their academicals "in public," a requirement that students found particularly irksome and which they quickly devised ways of evading.

The founders were also well aware that what they were creating at Trinity was in many respects very different from the other institutions of higher learning that were struggling along in the province. Though all colleges agreed that religion should form an important part of their institutional life, none enforced this commandment to the same extent as Trinity College. The University of Toronto claimed to cultivate a strong religious atmosphere, but it rejected the assertion that such an atmosphere demanded a direct tie to a specific church, let alone daily indoctrination in a particular creed. Furthermore, those colleges like Queen's and Victoria that retained their church affiliation did not exclude students who were members of other denominations. The college was also set apart by the internal life that the founders so carefully constructed. They put enormous store in the social and moral value of a college that was "strictly residential," and Strachan himself readily acknowledged that Trinity was more formal and regulated in this regard.[86] But others outside the college did not share their enthusiasm. There had been serious problems with the residences at Upper Canada College (perhaps explaining why so much concern was taken with enforcing discipline at Trinity College), and Egerton Ryerson, Strachan's former nemesis, questioned the moral consequences of forcing young men to live together in halls of residence while they were attending educational institutions away from home. He argued that the religious and moral goals of higher education were better served by having students board with their masters or in the homes of God-fearing Christians; in effect, to live with real families rather than surrogate ones.[87]

And finally the world the founders created within Trinity College also marked a clear departure from the social and cultural practices of earlier Anglican institutions in the colony. Although the Diocesan Theological Institute at Cobourg was an exclusively Anglican community overseen by a clergyman, the social and cultural life of the institute marched to the beat of a very different drummer. These prospective clergy were not treated like young children and forced to live in such a monastic and restrictive environment. Here there were no student residences or legislated codes of behaviour: students were free to establish their own households (some with servants) or board with families in the town.[88] They saw themselves as mature people and citizens of some importance in their local community. They aspired to be independent gentlemen, who could see to their own interests and were quite capable of living dispassionate, rational, and happy lives. And at night they did not need to rely on someone else to put them to bed. Needless to say, when these young gentlemen left Cobourg for Trinity College they encountered a very different social world.

The completed structure: Trinity College without additions, 1852 to 1877

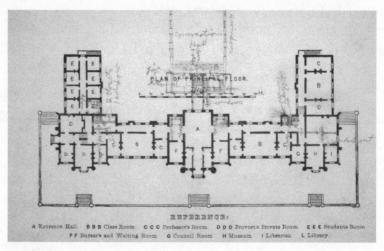

Plan of the principal floor

A Gothic perspective: The view of the chapel from the ravine

The view from Queen Street

"A university worthy of the name." Copy of the letter sent to the Trinity Committee in London by Bishop Strachan

First provost and guardian of the founding vision. Portrait of
Provost George Whitaker by Robert Harris

"Not only first rate men as Scholars but of very gentlemanly bearing and courteous manners."

Left: The Revd E. St John Parry, first professor of classics

Below: The Revd George Clerk Irving, first professor of mathematics

THE

CALENDAR

OF THE

University of Trinity College,

TORONTO,

FOR THE YEAR OF OUR LORD

1853.

TORONTO:

HENRY ROWSELL.

1853.

University of Trinity College.

THE UNIVERSITY OF TRINITY COLLEGE was constituted by a Royal Charter, bearing date 16th July 1852, and empowered to confer Degrees in Divinity, Arts, Law, and Medicine.

THE CONVOCATION of the University consists of the Chancellor, the Provost and Professors of Trinity College, and all persons admitted to the Degree of Master of Arts, or to any Degree in Divinity, Law, or Medicine, in the University.

No Degree can be granted by the University unless a Supplicat for that Degree shall have passed the Convocation, having been previously approved by the Caput.

THE CAPUT will consist of the Vice Chancellor; the Deans of the Faculties of Law and Medicine; and Two Masters of Arts, to be elected annually by Convocation at the first meeting in the Michaelmas Term.

The University confers no Degree whatever unless the Candidate has previously taken the oath of allegiance and supremacy and subscribed the following declaration:

"I A. B. do willingly and heartily declare that I am truly and sincerely a member of the United Church of England and Ireland."*

---

* For any Degree in Divinity, subscription to the Three Articles of the XXXVIth. Canon is also required.

"I am truly and sincerely a member of the United Church of England and Ireland." *The Calendar of the University of Trinity College, Toronto* (1853)

3

The Great Christian Household

Even before Trinity College opened its doors Bishop Strachan had already clothed this child of his later years in the language of domesticity, drawing an analogy between the college and a family to explain the true character of this nascent institution. When he wrote to the Trinity committee in London, he declared that the entire institution was to be organized "on the principle of the whole constituting one large family."[1] Provost Whitaker was then able to turn the same metaphor to his own advantage and assume effective mastery over the domestic life of the institution. If the college was a home and the community within it a family, he asserted, then students and servants should be responsible to "their ordinary superiors" – that is the provost and the professors, rather than the bishop of Toronto and the college council.[2] At the laying of the cornerstone and later at the opening of the college, Bishop Strachan once again drew on the metaphor of the family to describe not only the character of the college but its educational goals: "It will constitute a great Christian household, the domestic home of all who resort to it for instruction, framing them in the Christian graces, and in all sound learning, and sanctifying their knowledge, abilities and attainments to the service of God and the welfare of their fellow-men."[3]

When the founders described their college as a household or family, they were using an analogy that many other educators at that time had used to explain the character and the social role of schooling. Indeed Robert Gidney and Wyn Millar have asserted that the belief that schools were extensions of families and subordinate to them was a "fundamental assumption in shaping the structure of Upper Canadian education." Alison Prentice has in turn argued convincingly that families and schools were drawn together so frequently because mid-Victorian society had yet to draw a clear boundary between these two institutions. Both were regarded as important centres of learning that shared the same social and moral goals. Consequently, the roles of parents and teachers were invariably run together, indeed they were often mentioned in the same breath.[4] John Strachan, one of the most important educators in the history of Upper Canada, was well aware of this rhetorical practice, and the words he spoke at such important occasions must have been reassuringly familiar to his audiences.

But the founders of Trinity College pushed this analogy even farther by using the family in a more philosophical and pedagogical manner to explain aspects of the college that they believed (and perhaps feared) the public might not otherwise appreciate. At the opening ceremonies, for example, Bishop Strachan developed the analogy between college and family at some length to highlight two primary, and closely related, educational goals. First, he used the family to explain how true knowledge is acquired. He asked, in effect, a rhetorical question: where do students learn best those things it was most important for them to know? Education, he then answered, began in the family; indeed during the innocence of early childhood children not only learned their lessons effortlessly, but those lessons were enormously important, for they would shape their characters, especially their moral characters, for the rest of their lives. Here the bishop drew a pleasing portrait of a mother and her children, describing "the Holy Truths communicated and the first accents of prayer which a pious and tender mother whispered in [her children's] ears, invoking the protection of God and Saviour before she kissed them and consigned them to their night's repose."[5]

How noble and inspiring was this image of the mother as the moral centre of the family and the first (and best) teacher of her children! But what was truly remarkable here was the spiritual and pedagogical lessons the bishop drew from this family portrait. If such "Holy Truths" were best taught in childhood, then Trinity College must recapture this magical period of youthful innocence: "Now one of our principal objects in this Institution will be to bring back to the hearts and affections of our youth the fresh and innocent impressions of early infancy."[6] In effect, Trinity was to be patterned after a family in the hope that it would be able to institutionalize that period of life when students (like young children) could acquire, almost without thinking, those moral values that would shape their lives long after they had left this hallowed asylum. "We wish our young men to feel the beautiful and affecting influence of the pure example of little children."[7] The metaphor was not merely a rhetorical device; now the family was being held up quite self-consciously as a model for college life. This model was to be followed religiously.

This determination to institutionalize the "beautiful and affecting" innocence of youth had to contend, however, with a rather unfortunate truth. All these future leaders of church and state were at some distance removed from the age when moral lessons could be implanted almost effortlessly in their minds. The students the college gathered within its gates, Strachan pointed out, were young men between the ages of sixteen and twenty-two who, if left to their own devices, would gladly surrender whatever innocence they might have unwittingly retained. Certainly the bishop feared that if these students were "cast loose in a large city" where they would live on their own and be left free to choose their hours and companions, they would "fall prey to every corruption."[8] Trinity may have yearned to return these students to the angelic pleasures of a mother's nightly embrace; but this walled garden of academe was at the moment filled with somewhat lower primates whose passions threatened the educational and moral goals of the college.

At this point Strachan turned to matters of discipline and regulation: "In regard to discipline we cannot surely be required, in 1852, to shew that it is unnecessary, – on the contrary, the experience of all ages and countries points out the advantages of subjecting the passionate and enthusiastic period of youth to salutary control, as well as the great difficulty of rendering it effectual."[9] He then outlined the advantages that Trinity would gain by introducing "a steady and just system of control, firmly but affectionately exercised." Such a system would remove temptation from those who were weak; it would restrain those who were vicious and prevent "habits of vice by watchful supervision"; and it would threaten those who persist in evil with "the certainty" that they would "at length be discovered, condemned, disgraced and expelled."[10]

The real question for Strachan, however, was how to implement such a system, and make it work: "the great difficulty of rendering it effectual." For a second time Strachan pressed the analogy of the family into service. Families, he declared, not only provided the best setting for moral formation; they also afforded constructive models of proper social relations and effective discipline. They were natural hierarchies in which wisdom and authority flowed down from above while respect and obedience rose up from below. "Our desire then is to ... form ourselves, in as far as may be practicable, to the order and economy of a well regulated family."[11] And again these ideas were put into practice as the college proceeded through statutes, rules, and regulations to render such "salutary control" effectual. As we have seen, for the first three decades of its life Trinity College was marked by elaborate social distinctions held together by a strict, almost monastic discipline. Students gave way to professors, junior academics gave way to those more senior, and everyone deferred by virtue of his academic and clerical office to the provost, who assumed the same position in the college that the bishop enjoyed in the church and the father in the family. "Our discipline," he concluded, "partakes much of domestic control."[12] In fact, discipline and order were the watchwords of college life.[13]

The choice of such words and phrases was not accidental. The founders used the language of domesticity and the family because it served a number of useful purposes. By referring to a familiar social group in which growth and order seemed to work in perfect harmony, they were able to draw learning and discipline together and create an environment that would regulate freedom and channel knowledge towards useful moral goals.[14] Like the family, this well-regulated collegiate household could discipline the passions and enthusiasms of youth and so create an environment in which all these young men, like the children in a family, could learn the proper lessons of life not only from their surrogate parents but also from each other, both as children of their instructors and as brothers of their fellow students. Strachan, who idolized this type of education, attached enormous importance to the unique ability of a community *as a community* to foster moments of spiritual awakening. "There will also be among the young men themselves an affectionate brotherhood, confidential and salutary companionship, noble resolutions, aspiring hopes, useful conversation and friendly intimacy, on terms and with an intensity which nothing but a College life will admit."[15]

The comparison with families also helped the founders address the important matter of safety. It must be remembered that at this time in English-speaking Canada the benefits of educating young men by shutting them up together in a boarding hall regulated by a severe religious discipline were by no means obvious. In fact there were other ways of describing the college – for example, as a monastic community of learning – that would have been more accurate, but which also had Popish and other highly dangerous associations. So by linking higher education to home and family the founders were able to surround their new project with words and images that were familiar, easily understood, and safe – ones that claimed for Trinity College the virtually sacred authority that Victorians were coming to invest in a particular form of domestic relations. The analogy of the family reassured parents about the kind of education their sons would receive and the safety of the institution in which their enlightenment would take place. "It will gladden the hearts of their parents," Strachan explained, "to know that, though not immediately under their watchful eye, everything will be done to supply the place of paternal counsel and maternal tenderness."[16] Not only did the metaphor present the educational philosophy of the college in a language the public would understand, but it also made what went on behind the walls of old Trinity appear at once sound and safe.

Embedded in all these references to the college as a family, however, are two rather different conceptions of family life. These differences help us to understand the different ways in which Trinity was "educating" its students and preparing them for the larger world. In the first instance Strachan represented Trinity as a large extended family that was carefully organized by rank and social position, a family led by a great public figure that over time had assumed a prominent role in the life of the nation. The founder, for example, drew a direct analogy between the internal life of Trinity College and "a large family, under a like discipline, as to regularity and order, as distinguished the great households in England a century ago."[17]

This image of an eighteenth-century aristocratic household served in many ways as an apt model for the social world Trinity was trying to create. As we have noted the college clearly resembled such a large, extended family in which every member, from the bishop in his palace to the Irish serving girls below stairs, was placed within a carefully ranked hierarchy and made to conform to a "like discipline." The founders also believed that such a family expressed the relationship that the college was trying to establish with the outside world. Like the eighteenth-century family, the family of Trinity College would become an important part of Canadian public life. Once again we have seen how from the moment of its founding the college cultivated a close relationship with what Strachan regarded as the true social and political elite of Canadian society, anticipating that the college graduates would become "leading men in society as Clergymen, Lawyers, Physicians, Statesmen, Merchants and Landed Proprietors."[18] Indeed this public presence led Provost Whitaker to tell the divinity students that it was their duty to continue to perform the same public role that had made them – at least in theory – such valued members of this hierarchical social system. Using words that were drawn directly from Bishop Warburton, the provost told these prospective clergy that it was their primary duty as clergy to "urge the law of God upon the consciences of men." Thus the people would not only become "good Christians," but also "good citizens, and honest, sober men."[19] In effect, the college was organized like a large extended family in the hope that its graduates could step effortlessly into the highest stratum of a public world that shared the same social, cultural, and religious values; their presence would then reinforce the values and structure of this world.

This way of using the term "family" – extended, hierarchical, public, and patriarchal – evokes another family with which the founder of Trinity College had been intimately connected. Let us recall for a moment that hoary phrase from our colonial past, the Family Compact. By the 1830s this slogan had acquired such political force because it employed the same notion of a large extended family to challenge the way power and privilege were organized and distributed in Upper Canada. The term referred to a group of men who were bound together, not by any biological relationship, but by the "like discipline" they shared – the class position, social attitudes, political interests, and religious beliefs they held in common. And, for friend and foe alike the term defined a clear relationship between such a "family" and real political and social power. Indeed, the phrase was so effective as a political slogan precisely because it captured the truth that the yeomanry of Upper Canada found so irksome – that membership in this extended family was a direct path to public office, a secure income, and high social standing. The Anglican religious establishment, of course, was very much a part of the Family Compact, and it should come as no surprise that the reformers' condemnation of the compact was also directed against the privileges enjoyed by the state church. In the raw democracy of Upper Canada, the reformers argued, power and authority should be the reward for honest labour and good conduct, not the gift of patronage and family connections.[20]

Lord Durham's *Report*, which foretold the demise of both the Family Compact and the established church, envisaged a new social order in which the colonial state would cultivate the self-interest of entrepreneurs and promote the rapid economic development of the colony.[21] As we have seen, the church responded to these changes by creating a new institutional structure that gave it complete control over its own affairs. It created a sacred, private asylum that was set apart from this new threatening world.

The search for asylum – a place that was private, set apart, and morally pure – was also conveyed in the second, more domestic notion of the family that Strachan used in describing the character of college life. The eighteenth-century household that Strachan had appealed to was extended, public, hierarchical, and patriarchal; but he also represented the college as a small, essentially private group of people bound together by a close biological relationship. This family was described as a moral asylum that was set apart from the secular world, and it was distinguished, not by the headship of a powerful male public figure, but by the tender care of a loving mother whose innate moral nature gave her an unrivalled place in the religious upbringing of her children. Here the language of paternal discipline and order gave way to the voice of maternal kindness and moral education: "the Holy Truths communicated and the first accents of prayer which a pious and tender mother whispered in [her children's] ears, invoking the protection of God and Saviour before she kissed them and consigned them to their night's repose."[22]

This second image of the family, as small, private, female-centred, biologically related, and moral, also illuminated important social and educational themes in the cultural construction of Trinity College. The college may have liked to describe itself as a patriarchal aristocratic household, but some of the leading members of this collegiate household were expressing genuine concern about the growing distance between the world inside Trinity College and the social world that was developing outside. When Provost Whitaker encouraged his clergy to take up the same public role they had played in the old colonial establishment, he also cautioned them that once they left the college they would enter a world that was very different from the one they had known. In the old hierarchical world of church and state, the clergy could rely upon the support and protection of the state as well as the legal and social authority they enjoyed as professional gentlemen. But in the present dispensation, they must "urge the law of god upon the consciences of men, unsupported by the authority of human law or public opinion." How can we find solace in the laws of the state, Whitaker lamented, when those laws often appear "selfish rather than benevolent, made for others' good rather than our own?"[23]

In much the same way that the Family Compact had lost its political position to the representatives of new social and economic interests, so too the authority of an exclusive Anglican elite closely linked to the state was giving way to a middle-class Protestant culture tied to the very material world of commercial and industrial development.[24] How were the clergy to act in this new world? What authority could they now rely on as they tried to carry out their social duty when appeals to social position and the state carried so little weight? Whitaker's answer is revealing. In this new age, he argued, the clergy had to rely almost entirely on their inherent moral authority, on the ability of their strong and unblemished moral characters to place them on a pedestal of authority that few others in society could rival. This was the theme Whitaker returned to time and again in the sermons he preached in the college chapel: "Let us bear in mind, therefore, that for the highest and holiest service in which God employs us on earth, the qualifications are of different kinds, partly intellectual and partly moral, and that the moral are the weightier; that, so far as we can judge, the latter were chiefly regarded by our Lord in His choice of the twelve." The clergy should be educated, they should be gentlemanly, but above all else they must display that high moral character that would allow them to shine as beacons of truth to a corrupted world.[25]

The fact that Trinity College set out to recreate a culture of childlike innocence in order to implant such moral values in all its students is evidence of the immense weight that was coming to be placed in a college education on the formation of a strong moral character. While the college curriculum was based on the acquisition of knowledge and the attainment of a bachelor's degree – a degree that marked one's high status within a social hierarchy – the internal life of the college, organized and regulated so carefully to recreate and protect those moments of childhood innocence, was intended to instill something rather different. The lessons learned at a mother's knee had little to do with the classical curriculum and the three examination fences a young gentleman had to clear to pass out of Trinity College. Mothers did not teach their children the rules for mastering the imperfect tense in Latin;[26] rather they taught them to be good and implanted in them a moral code that would regulate, as if by instinct, their behaviour for the rest of their lives. And it is Trinity's devotion to the necessity of moral formation within the university that the metaphor of the maternal family was intended to convey.

In placing such store in the acquisition of a strong moral character, Trinity College was also participating in a much broader cultural movement. As scholars of religion have pointed out, by the middle of the nineteenth century institutional religion as a whole was expressed increasingly in the language of domesticity and moral character. A. Gregory Schneider has argued cogently that Methodism adopted the language of home and domesticity in order to challenge the power that traditional religious elites enjoyed in the public sphere – a development that suggests a fascinating comparison to the Anglican Church, which was also trying to find in the family a new cultural identity as it was losing the public position it had recently enjoyed. So powerful and widespread was this appeal to moral character and the family that one suspects that many members of the respectable middle classes were adopting the notion that morality and religion were much the same thing and that the small nuclear family was not only the very embodiment of these values but their missioner as well.[27]

Once again many elements of this pedagogy may seem commonplace, or even suspiciously natural; it takes a certain courage to express doubts about the value of a sound moral character. Certainly, few at that time would have questioned the notion that a good education included moral formation, or that a woman's distinctive moral nature gave her a special role to play in this process, or the idea that moral formation should begin at an early age. Nevertheless, one can still raise serious questions about the way these assumptions combined at Trinity College. Mothers may well have had an important part to play in the moral education of young children, but at Trinity this notion was to serve as one of the building blocks of the new collegiate community. Trinity set about to recreate a period of youthful innocence in order to retrieve those childhood moments when such motherly moral formation took place most effectively. By the same token one could readily accept the need for order and discipline in education without surrounding this collegiate community with an elaborate set of rules designed to restrict the freedom and experiences of the young scholars.

The most telling critique of this world of innocence and regulation came in fact from the students themselves. Far from accepting the environment in which they were forced to live, they confronted the founders' educational ideals and challenged directly what was going on behind the walls of old Trinity. The very first men of college, those who had come up to Trinity from the Diocesan

Theological Institute in Cobourg, bridled at the restrictions this new collegiate world imposed on their freedom and the way it refused to acknowledge their social position. They despised being treated like children, and their testimony speaks volumes about the founding culture of Trinity College:

> Most of us had come from a small town where, as students of Divinity, we had been thought persons of some consequence to the Church and to society, and were very much our own masters, and were regarded with much interest by our several boarding-house keepers. It was no small trial to us ... to be brought under strict domestic – almost monastic – discipline; to be put into a new and imperfectly warmed building in the dead of winter, and to be subjected to precise rules as to chapel and meals, and going out and coming in, and generally to more or less restriction of our liberty. The Steward, on whom so much depended, was decidedly crusty and sometimes tyrannical; and I remember well how annoyed some of us were when he spoke of us as 'the men' when we thought he should have said 'the gentlemen.'[28]

At Cobourg, ideas about character and discipline were expressed very differently. There the culture of education was shaped by a well-established tradition of apprenticeship training in which younger men worked closely with a senior member of their profession, acquiring skills and knowledge by imitating their elders. They were not subjected to a strict set of rules or enclosed in a secluded residential institution. They enjoyed enough freedom to set up their own institutions (which formed an important part of the cultural life of the town) and conducted their lives according to the gentlemanly world to which they aspired.[29] Both institutions were deeply concerned about character formation, but at each institution character formation meant something different, and the formation of character followed a different course. Trinity tended to regard character as a question of morality, the ability to act instinctively in a way that conformed to a religious and moral code. The institute at Cobourg, however, was disposed to associate character with virtue, the ability one acquired to put aside one's own interests and feelings, understand the complexity of a situation, and choose the path that would advance the higher good. To form a strong moral character, Trinity set about implanting in the young men a strong and unshakeable moral code that would allow them to react instinctively to the situations they would encounter throughout their lives. The institute at Cobourg, in contrast, assumed that virtue was the gift of age, reason, and experience: acting virtuously was a power one gained by acquiring knowledge and by studying and imitating the lives of those who had already learned to act in a virtuous manner. If Trinity celebrated the child, Cobourg believed there was a time to put away childish things.

Perhaps the presence of this older group of students (and the student-run institutions they brought with them from Cobourg) served as a counterweight to the world the founders were trying to create. Certainly their criticism of the college would be echoed by many of their fellow students. The men of college circulated petitions asking the college council to relax some of the more irksome rules, and when the council rejected their petitions, many students simply ignored the regulations and paid the resulting fines. One student, however, felt the full wrath of the institution because of an episode that highlights not only the restrictive, juvenile character of this collegiate family, but also the strong reaction it provoked.

A young member of a very prominent Toronto family, who in later life was to enjoy a considerable reputation as a police magistrate, military strategist, and advocate of imperial federation, had the misfortune to be caught scribbling during one of the Provost's divinity lectures. When he refused to yield up the offending scrap of paper, he was brought before the provost and ordered to apologize in writing for his unseemly behaviour. In time he submitted, but the provost rejected his apology – although it was signed by the penitent, it was not written out entirely in his own hand. At this point George Taylor Denison, Jr, was expelled even though his record in the college was exemplary and he was about to complete his ninth term and graduate. His father (who had marshalled the procession to the laying of the cornerstone) was outraged and published his correspondence with the provost in a pamphlet: "If the College is to be conducted upon the principles of Colleges at home, I contend that the students should be gentlemen, and if not gentlemen, they ought not to be there; but if gentlemen, then they are most certainly entitled to that courtesy which gentlemen have a right to expect from one another; and my son as a young gentleman, I contend, has not been treated as such by the Provost." There was no doubt in his mind that the internal life of the college was different from that of other institutions of higher learning, and that the unique characteristics of Trinity undermined the social goals that should guide a college education. For his part Provost Whitaker seems to have taken pride in his ability to face down "resolutely" the "unpopularity consequent on the maintenance of a strict clerical discipline."[30] The title of the pamphlet broadcast to the world beyond the gates a condemnation of the college that many members of this collegiate family undoubtedly shared: "Trinity College Conducted As a Mere Boys' School, Not As a College."[31]

This description of the college as "a mere boys' school" raises a fascinating speculation about another educational institution that may well have served as a model for Trinity College. Towards the end of his life Bishop Strachan reviewed his own extensive career in education. The first half of the nineteenth century had been a period of profound educational change. Schools and schooling were matters of intense public concern, and Strachan had not only taken a prominent part in such debates, but he had also been an active participant in the process of educational change itself as a teacher, administrator, and the founder of important educational institutions. He oversaw the development of state-supported schooling in Upper Canada, and he played a large part in the founding of three Canadian universities – King's College, Trinity, and McGill. But he did not compare himself to men such as Newman or Gladstone, who had helped to reshape theological and university education. Rather he compared his career to that of Thomas Arnold, the great headmaster of Rugby School. In fact, Strachan's writings reveal a deep interest in the ideas and policies of those headmasters who would transform the British public schools into national institutions. Strachan praised especially the way these institutions brought the church into the residential lives of their students.[32] There were several models for Trinity College. Strachan, who claimed that King's College was the founding model, dwelt on the necessity of maintaining the tie between religion and education; he drew on St Aidan's College, Birkenhead, for the architectural plans for his new college; and he acknowledged that Cambridge and Oxford provided the standard for the college curriculum. Given the founder's appeals to child-like innocence and the necessity of discipline (and the reaction such policies provoked), perhaps Rugby School had been the model for the domestic life of the University of Trinity College.

These attacks on the founding culture of Trinity were direct and seemingly straightforward: the students were gentlemen and should be treated as such. But the word "gentleman" is not only a class marker; it also defined this community in relation to gender. Not only was the college refusing to recognize the social status to which they aspired, but there was also something unmanly about the way in which the students were being treated. They were gentlemen, and gentlemen should not be treated like mere boys.

Matters surrounding gender and sexuality are among the most difficult for the historian to uncover. Such a heading never made it onto the agenda of the college council, and it is safe to assume that if there was any sexual scandal in the college, every effort would have been made to keep it out of public view. And yet problems related to the construction of gender – what type of men was Trinity creating – form a persistent leitmotif in many of the criticisms of the domestic world of Trinity College. These troubled the college almost from the moment of its inception and continued to plague it for many years.

Once again the way in which the college was being described as a "family" can help to bring these troubles to light. The metaphor of the family had been used to explain many aspects of college life, but in some ways it was not as apt as the founders believed. Embedded within this metaphor most notably were some rather unsettling ambiguities about the sexual dynamics of college life. As we have seen the metaphor of the family drew together two discreet functions – moral formation and discipline. But the bishop's language shifted significantly as he moved from the first of these objectives to the second. When speaking of the family as a moral economy, as a model for recapturing those moments of childhood innocence, Strachan described the college in explicitly feminine terms. He compared college education with a mother whom he described as the embodiment of moral wisdom, which she transmitted through love and affection. But when he turned to the family as an economy of discipline, he described the college in unmistakably masculine terms. It was "under the paternal roof" that the academic family could inflict on the students "a well regulated restraint for several years, during the most critical period of their lives."³³ And such restraint came about not through love and affection but from an elaborate set of rules and regulations strictly enforced by the professors in their roles as the male parents of the collegiate community.

The founder, in fact, ran these gendered educational roles together in the very same sentence. "Everything will be done," he explained at the inauguration ceremonies, "to supply the place of paternal counsel and maternal tenderness."³⁴ In effect, Strachan was asking those in authority in the collegiate family to carry out the male task of discipline and the female task of moral nurture. And it goes without saying that, except for the wife of the provost and the Irish serving girls, scarcely a woman was to be found within the gates of Old Trinity.

The fact that the professors in Trinity College were being called on to perform tasks increasingly associated with women raised questions about the "manliness" of these men as well as the character of the students they produced. Given the fact that all the professors were priests, these suspicions were largely directed at the teaching of divinity and the environment in which clerical education took place. Here the college was caught up in a broader attack on the type of education that was conducted in the new Tractarian seminaries in Britain, an attack in which the construction of gender figures very prominently. Beginning in the 1840s these seminaries had been established to prepare young men for ordination according to the new ideals of the priesthood put forward by the Oxford Movement. Like Trinity these had been set up by bishops, and they followed a monastic system in which university graduates were brought together in a closed community under close clerical supervision. Unlike Trinity, however, these institutions were not tied directly to a university and did not offer academic degrees.

In 1858, the bishop of Oxford's seminary, Cuddesdon College, was rocked by scandal when charges of homosexual practices led to the removal of the principal, the vice principal, and the college chaplain. This event was widely reported, and it confirmed for many a long-standing fear of both the content and the method of instruction that these high-church seminaries had adopted. Here, it was claimed, good Protestant youth were being corrupted in mind and body by being force-fed a steady diet of fancy ritualism and Roman dogma in a hothouse clerical atmosphere. Less than a year later the very same criticism of theological education and its implied sexual practices would be launched against Trinity College by Benjamin Cronyn, the first bishop of Huron. Remembered primarily as a largely unsubstantiated attack on the theological principles of Provost Whitaker, Cronyn's critique of Trinity mirrored almost exactly the way the evangelicals were attacking theological education in Britain. Criticizing both the methods Whitaker used and the content of his teaching, Bishop Cronyn charged that within the enclosed clerically controlled world of Trinity College, Whitaker was using "the Provost's catechism" to force-feed good Protestant youth with Roman doctrine. He and his supporters then filled their pamphlets with allusions whose sexual intentions were scarcely concealed. Indeed, one suspects that the provost, the college council, and Bishop Strachan went to such great lengths to defend the college because they were well aware of the devastating impact such charges had had in Britain.[35]

The evangelical critique of Trinity as a centre of "ritualism" followed the same lines as Cronyn's attack on theological education and played upon the same sexual ambiguities. The link between ritualism and femininity was obvious, and although the charge that Trinity during the Whitaker years was a hotbed of ritualism was quite unfounded, the sexual fears linked to this association must have done considerable damage. Certainly, the popular press took up this theme and seemed to enjoy dressing up the faculty of Trinity College in suspiciously feminine garb.[36] Questions of gender also figure prominently in the battle between the "high-church" and "evangelical" parties over theological education in the Diocese of Toronto.[37] Certainly the Protestant Episcopal Divinity School (which was soon renamed Wycliffe College) adopted a very different approach to clerical training and tried to project a very different image of the clergy it produced. Founded near the end of Whitaker's term, it rejected from the outset the enclosed monasticism of Trinity College. Instead it affiliated itself with the University of Toronto, not only so that its students could attend classes in arts, but also to be sure that these sound evangelical youth would not be entrapped in a clerically dominated environment. And the image of a Wycliffe man – a missionary battling evil on the frontiers of Christendom – was decidedly more muscular than the altar-centred, inwardly focused priest associated with Trinity College. Once again it must be pointed out that no evidence has been found to support these criticisms and their implications. At the same time there is no doubt that the image of a priest that Provost Whitaker liked to hold aloft in his sermons – an aesthetic and detached figure of unblemished moral character whose high spiritual calling barred him from enjoying even the mildest of manly pleasures – was intended to be an alternative to the popular, and more aggressive, conceptions of manliness.[38]

There is another dimension to the question of sexual ambiguity that would affect the history of Trinity College. When the assertion that Trinity was a family dedicated to the moral formation of its students was combined with the notion that moral formation was a role for which women had a special gift, then women found in their hands a powerful weapon for challenging centuries of male privilege in both religion and higher education. If religion was primarily about teaching people to lead a moral life, and education was a process of moral formation, how then could women – universally acknowledged as the moral superiors of men – be excluded from either the church or the university?[39] This was by no means the only argument women would use to open the doors of Trinity College, nor did this claim to a special moral nature ensure that once inside they would be granted a position of equality. As Brian Heeney has pointed out, women were able to expand their sphere within the church, but their sphere was always ranked below the one controlled by men.[40] The same was true at Trinity; although the motion that admitted women was a ringing endorsement of academic equality within Trinity – that "women be admitted to the degrees in any faculty on complying with the conditions prescribed by Statute and Bylaw"[41] – the college continued for over a century to ponder what equality actually meant. Nonetheless, the admission of women was a triumph over the all-male world Whitaker had constructed. Within two years of his departure this founding doctrine was simply cast aside.[42]

These challenges, which concerned the way the family of Trinity College had been constructed, came for the most part from within the college family itself. The men of college had fought against the restrictive social environment the founders had created, and gradually they established a strong student culture with its own institutions, games, and rituals. The challenge by women to the all-male world of Trinity College was strongly supported by lay members of the college council, especially the Henderson brothers, as well as the new provost, the members of the board of Bishop Strachan School, and the headmistress of that institution, the redoubtable Miss Rose Grier.[43] But the strongest challenge to the college came, not from inside, but from the groups and ideas that had purposely been excluded.

Policies of exclusions were taken very seriously at Trinity College. When it created an exclusively Anglican community, the college turned away all sorts of people – Presbyterians, Methodists, and Baptists, not to mention Catholics, Jews, and free thinkers, in fact all those who were not prepared to declare, in order to take a degree, that they were "truly and sincerely a member of the United Church of England and Ireland."[44] We have also encountered some of the problems that resulted from such a policy of exclusion. In 1856 when Provost Whitaker refused to relax any of these restrictions, the entire Faculty of Medicine resigned, arguing that it was impossible to conduct a medical school with such a narrow base from which to draw both students and faculty.[45]

In many respects the policy of exclusion was based on a simple ideological and financial calculation. In purposefully excluding all these groups, Trinity College was forgoing any possibility that any of these groups would support the college directly. How after all could one seriously contemplate appealing to a Methodist for support when young Methodists would only be admitted on the assumption that they would give up their religious enthusiasms. There was, however, a positive side to this strategy: because Trinity was a purely Anglican college, it could make a strong claim upon the members of its own denomination. The college had been founded for their benefit alone, and membership has its responsibilities.

But this exchange – excluding others in return for strong support from the members of the church – simply did not work. The church in Britain, as we have seen, had expressed its determination to support the colonial church in other parts of the Empire, although this fact did not stop Trinity trying to appeal (and not without success) to the SPG for money. Far more unsettling, especially over the longer term, was the stark fact that many Anglicans in Canada refused to come forward and support the college, or only supported it for a short time.

In general the clergy supported Trinity College, although it should come as no surprise that Bishop Cronyn and his band of evangelicals (now well ensconced in the Diocese of Huron) refused to do so. In fact their attack on Whitaker and his teaching was clearly intended to channel money and students destined for Trinity to Cronyn's own institution, Huron College.[46] Nonetheless, Trinity could count on broad support among the clergy, and even more support as the college prepared more and more men for the church.

The lay members of the church, however, were quite another matter. Right from its founding, Trinity had been unable to obtain the support of a prominent group of Anglican laity in the Diocese of Toronto. When Trinity was founded, Peter Boyle De Blaquiere, a prominent Anglican who was the chancellor of the new University of Toronto, had offered his support to the college if Trinity limited itself to the teaching of divinity. The way would then be clear for Trinity to affiliate with the provincial institution. Strachan, of course, refused, and Trinity began as a full university and a rival to the provincial university. With the founding of Trinity College, however, De Blaquiere and his friends did not simply admit defeat and leave education to Bishop Strachan and Trinity College. This powerful and well-connected group of Anglican evangelicals not only refused to support Trinity, but they continued to be strong supporters of the University of Toronto, and in time they founded and financed Trinity's other arch-rival, Wycliffe College.[47]

By excluding non-Anglicans, Trinity began with a very restricted base of support; its failure to accommodate this important group of Anglican evangelicals reduced its base even further. Nowhere was this problem felt more acutely than in the area of finance. From the beginning, the financial position of the college had been weak. Although on paper the initial appeal in Canada had been quite successful – £31,607 was subscribed in the province – ten years later £10,000 was still owing in unpaid sub-scriptions. Furthermore, much of what had been collected was in the form of unsold land whose value was subject to the fluctuations in the provincial economy.[48] When the college finally hired a competent person to assess the value of the college's land holdings, it was informed by Mr J.W. Whitney that except for lot no. 12 in Enniskillen Township (which was at the centre of an oil boom), most of the college land was of little value and some of it quite worthless. As long as the college continued to hold the land, however, it was obliged to pay taxes on it, which of course drained the value of the endowment.[49] The other source of college revenue – the income from student fees – also presented a real problem. Revenues here were based on a very optimistic projection of an enrol-ment of about fifty students, but once again the fact that the college had excluded all non-Anglicans gave the college a limited basis upon which to draw students. Enrolments continually fell below the mark and only rose when Whitaker's successor abol-ished thses restrictions. And the whole strategy was vulnerable to the economic cycle, which could drive down the value of the endowment and the number of students at the same time.

The founder was again very blunt: "At present the income of the College is by no means sufficient to meet current expenses."[50] The college continued to respond to these financial crises by drawing on the endowment, and when this was not enough, it cut costs (students would have to pay for their own beer) and in-creased student fees, in this case to £50 for board and £12/10 for classes.[51] Enrolments, however, were already falling from the recent downturn in the economy, and this move reduced them even further. The college responded by laying off staff and reduc-ing the professors' salaries.

A second problem bedevilled college finances. Not only was the college trying to survive on a very narrow financial base, but it was handicapped by the curiously eighteenth-century inheritance in which its financial sensibilities seemed to languish. On the one hand the founders clearly understood the need to appeal to the members of the church for money; and Strachan, for one, acknowledged their importance by allowing the contributors to the college to elect six members to the Provisional Council. The creation of Convocation – a body that all Trinity graduates could join upon the payment of 20s a year – also brought members of the laity into the life of the college. And yet the college did not seem to appreciate the full implications of their presence, especially in view of the changes that were taking place in Canadian society. Once the buildings were up and a reasonable endowment in place (at least on paper), the college seemed to assume that finances would largely look after themselves. The endowment would see to salaries while student fees could cover everything else. The laity, who had given generously, could now be safely put to one side, at least until the next financial crisis. And then the college seems to have assumed that appeals should be directed (at least in the first instance) to its own professional elite, to those Anglican members of the learned professions the church regarded as the natural leaders of society. When Strachan was trying to deal with one of these financial crises, he had simply turned to "six gentlemen" who "had promised me 1,000 pounds each and many half that sum."[52] But his friends failed him.

By the mid-Victorian period, wealth and power were passing increasingly into the hands of a new commercial and industrial class, which was building a bourgeois society that was rather different from the one envisaged by Trinity. This class included many influential Anglican evangelicals (who had no problems mastering the mysteries of commerce and finance). Blinded by its own social assumptions, the college seemed to pass over the broad base of church members, some of whom had helped the college in its early days. The Gooderham family, for example, had given money to Trinity and taken an active part in the early history of the college. Once the Provisional Council had taken control of the college, however, the Gooderham name disappears from the college records, only to appear among the supporters of Wycliffe College.[53]

Another residue of the old order also did serious injury to both the church and Trinity College. Finances, it appears, were entrusted to men who did not merit such trust, or to put the matter more generously, being a gentleman and a member of the United Church of England and Ireland were regarded as sufficient proof of financial skill and moral probity. This proved to be a serious mistake. In 1852 the church discovered that Thomas Champion, a man who had served the church in a number of important financial positions and who at that time was secretary of the college, had been "swindling the Church Society out of its Funds for some time past."[54] He was quickly replaced by Charles McGrath, but not before his name and title (*T. Champion Collegii Scriniarius*) were inscribed on the brass plate that was placed on the cornerstone of the old college (and is now set in the main entrance to the college building). In later years both a bursar and a chancellor (a prominent lawyer and politician who had been entrusted with the care of the commutation funds) also fell rather short of this gentlemanly standard by failing to separate their own financial interests from those of the college and the church. Their failures would (once again) place both the church and the college in a very difficult position.[55]

The most disturbing challenge to Trinity College, however, was to come from the Anglican Church itself. When Peter Boyle De Blaquiere was sparring with Strachan over the founding of Trinity, he had asked the bishop a frightening question: "I am not aware that our Church, as such, has ever been consulted, or has applied for such an Institution."[56] Strachan had proclaimed that Trinity College was a church university, but on whose authority was he making this claim? The same question was also raised in synod, the institution that had been founded at the same time as Trinity as part of a common response to the dismemberment of the old alliance of church and state. It must then have struck fear into the friends of Trinity College when in 1872 the Revd J.W.R. Beck, a well-respected member of synod, rose from his seat and launched a devastating attack on the college. Beck was no crazed evangelical obsessed with papal conspiracies; he was the rector of Peterborough and a graduate of the Diocesan Theological Institute in Cobourg. He had also studied law before turning to the church, and his memorial to synod was drawn up with the precision and analytical detail for which he was famous.[57]

His critique of Trinity consisted of sixteen points: a charge supported by fifteen detailed assertions.[58] He concentrated on enrolment, finance, governance, and the relationship between the college, the synod, and the church. In twenty years, he claimed, only 120 students had "passed through the College and taken their degree ... an average of six students per year." Over a third of the parishes and stations in the Diocese of Toronto had not given any financial support to the college, nor had Trinity taken any steps to provide information about the college to the parishes or the diocese as a whole. Finally, he portrayed the council of Trinity College as a distant and unresponsive body that was not representative of the community it was supposed to serve. In effect, the college was a closed corporation that was governed and administered by a clerical elite, which took no interest in the broader issues facing the church. All this was brought together in his general charge, which in many respects was just as devastating as the one launched by the students themselves: "Trinity College

... does not command the confidence and support of the members of the Church in the Province of Ontario."[59]

At the founding ceremonies, Bishop Strachan had argued that religion must not be separated from higher education, and he attacked that godless abomination, the University of Toronto unceasingly. He then set about to build a college that eschewed such dangerous notions and that proclaimed at every opportunity its devotion to God, sound learning, and the Anglican Church. It is clear that Strachan took his own critique very seriously, for he had placed religion at the centre of the college curriculum, and a strong clerical ethos pervaded the entire life of the college. But he did not stop there. After all, the assertion that religion should be the cornerstone of the curriculum and that clergy should oversee the social and academic life of a college would have been acknowledged by almost everyone in Canada West. What set Trinity apart was Strachan's refusal to separate the college from the institutional structure of a church. The University of Toronto appealed to a broad body of Christian values that were not tied to a particular religious group; although a "secular" college, it espoused a common Christianity that it believed all denominations could share. Trinity College specifically rejected the notion that religion (and education) could exist apart from a church. "It is not in the nature of things," Strachan wrote, "that confidence and respect can ever attend a seat of learning, where if a church is spoken of it must be a church without Government, and where religion is taught it must be religion without doctrine."[60] For this reason the governance, the curriculum, the professors, and the internal life of Trinity College were all tied by bonds of membership, doctrine, ordination, and worship to the United Church of England and Ireland. Indeed, the founders hoped to build upon this fundamental distinction, throwing down a direct challenge to the new secular state. As more and more church grammar schools were "received into Union with the College," they joyfully looked forward to the day when Trinity would become the crowning glory of a complete Anglican alternative to the secular system of public instruction.[61] This was the mast to which the founders had tied the college colours: Trinity was a church college, and on this conviction it would either stand or fall.

Less than five years after the founder's death, a clergyman from Peterborough in the backwoods of Upper Canada would, in effect, speak out in the midst of that same church and make the one assertion that would reveal just how precarious the college's position actually was: "Trinity College does not command the support of the members of the Church in the Province of Ontario."

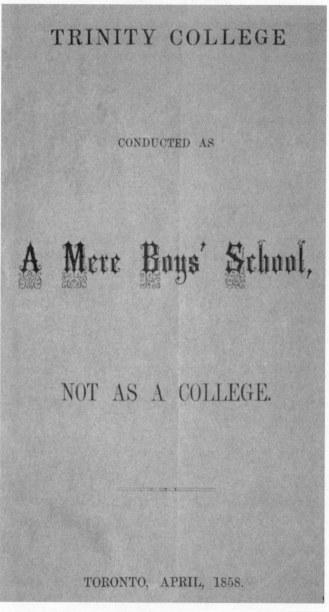

A challenge to the established order: Trinity College a mere boys' school

STRICTURES

ON THE

TWO LETTERS OF PROVOST WHITAKER

IN ANSWER TO CHARGES BROUGHT

BY THE

LORD BISHOP OF HURON

AGAINST THE

TEACHING OF TRINITY COLLEGE.

BY A PRESBYTER.

LONDON, C. W.:
PRINTED BY THOMAS EVANS, DUNDAS STREET EAST.
1861.

A challenge to the teaching of Trinity College

A place for women: St Hilda's College (Eden Smith, architect, 1899)

New course, new history: Portrait of Provost C.W.E. Body by
E. Wyly Grier

Epilogue
Refounding Trinity College

John Strachan, *fundator noster,* died on All Saints Day 1867, in the ninetieth year of life, the sixty-fifth year of his ministry, and the twenty-ninth year of his episcopate.[1] In many ways Alexander Neil Bethune and George Whitaker, the other two men who had played such prominent roles in the founding and early history of the college, continued to live in the founder's shadow. Strachan regarded both men as his sons, and they expressed their filial devotion by protecting and nurturing the college he left to their care without wavering from the principles on which it had been founded. Bethune succeeded Strachan as bishop of Toronto, and from this position continued to serve the college by participating actively in the deliberations of the college council, ordaining the candidates presented by the college (and overseeing their advancement in the church), and defending the college from attacks in synod and from the newly formed Wycliffe College.

For his part Provost Whitaker was determined to defend the founder's vision by guarding the character of the college from within. His success can be measured by the remarkable constancy found in every important aspect of college life. During his term the college scarcely changed architecturally. The building on Queen Street was intended to form the south side of a substantial academic quadrangle, and several times the college council tried to complete the original design by adding new residences and classrooms, a chapel, a library, and a convocation hall. But these plans were never carried out. Even the appeal to build a library and convocation hall "as a memorial to the Founder" failed for lack of financial support and had to be abandoned a year later.[2] Except for the convocation hall that was opened at the very end of Whitaker's career (it was funded by a special gift),[3] the college in 1881 consisted of the single building it had begun with thirty years before.[4]

Throughout this period, students, professors, and the members of the council were still required to affirm publicly their allegiance to the United Church of England and Ireland. The relaxation of these tests in 1871 in order to permit the return of the medical faculty was phrased in such a way that it actually reaffirmed the exclusively Anglican character of the college. By compelling any one who wished to forgo this religious test to petition the chancellor individually, the provost was able to reaffirm the general practice of imposing religious tests. At the same time council took special pains to state that these very limited indulgences were intended to increase "the influence of the College, as a Church of England institution" and did not alter in any way "the studies or discipline of the College."[5]

The "studies and discipline" that the council was intent on preserving affirm once again the determination of Provost Whitaker to hold to the course laid out at the founding. The rules and regulations enshrined in 1851 still welcomed the students who entered the college thirty years on. As in the matter of religious tests, Whitaker was prepared to give way on a few small matters in order to protect the "strict clerical discipline" of college life.[6] Simple fines replaced gatings as the preferred punishment, and after repeated requests he finally agreed to relax some of the most irksome regulations, such as the rule requiring all students to wear the cap and gown whenever they stepped outside the college grounds.[7] But these were minor modifications that had almost no effect on the internal life of the college. The laws governing the residence, the dining hall, and the chapel remained firmly in force, and the college continued to be run in the image of a well-disciplined Christian household.

Finally, and perhaps most important, the academic programme set down in 1851 seemed almost impervious to the winds of curricular reform. Over this period the college had taken a few hesitant steps in the seemingly radical direction of offering courses in a few new subjects – first in moral science, physiology, and chemistry, and later in French, fine art, and music. But with the notable exception of Dr Bovell's lectures in physiology and natural theology, all these additions were optional and largely ornamental. However popular these subjects were to become, during Whitaker's term they were never allowed to threaten the core of the curriculum. As they had in the beginning, students at Trinity earned their degrees by keeping terms and sitting examinations in divinity, classics, and mathematics.[8]

On Sunday, 20 June 1880 Provost George Whitaker preached his last sermon in the college chapel; the theme – the duty to remain true to the founder's vision – was a fitting tribute to his long and distinguished career. In the sermon he set out "to trace the history of the origin of this college; and, on that history, to base my own steadfast conviction of what its future ought to be."

His account of the history of the college, "unknown to some and forgotten by others," repeated the founding story that Bishop Strachan had first told thirty years before: the generous provisions of the Crown for education, the founding and early success of King's College, its fateful secularization on the first day of January 1850, and finally the steps taken by Bishop Strachan and the other founders to create a new college "to secure to the members of the Church of England" a college for "the religious education of their children." All this was presented in heroic terms.

Whitaker then asked "whether the position they achieved for us should be retained or abandoned." Here he took aim at those who were advocating federation with the provincial university. He admitted that if education was seen in purely secular terms, such a course had many advantages, but Trinity was a church college dedicated to "the transcendent importance of religious training." All its instruction, both sacred and secular, was tempered by faith, it prepared both the laity and the clergy for active roles in the church, and the college as a whole stood as a beacon of religious purity amid "the Proteus-like infidelity of the times." Those then were the "priceless benefits of such an education as can be given only on Christian principles, and under the hallowed shelter of the Church of Christ." His exhortation was forceful, eloquent, and clear: it was the duty of the college "faithfully to guard the trust committed to us to maintain [Trinity] as a Church university."[9]

The sermon reaffirmed the ideas and values that had guided his career. He had worked to create an enclosed, residential, hierarchical, and exclusively Anglican family, and he defended his vision of Trinity College to the end. But the sermon proved to be a eulogy for that vision. In fact, Whitaker's determination to hold fast to this course had pushed the college to the brink of collapse. The enterprise that had begun with so much pomp and splendour in 1851 was now under-enrolled, financially impoverished, challenged academically by new ideas, and increasingly isolated in the church it was supposed to represent. Even as Whitaker preached this last sermon, the council was formulating strategies, including federation, to solve these problems, and under Whitaker's successor these strategies would transform the college almost beyond recognition.

The course this transformation would run was somewhat circuitous, but its progress was at once rapid and complete. When Bishop Bethune died in 1879, Provost Whitaker quickly emerged as the favourite to succeed him as bishop of Toronto, for Whitaker had shown strongly in the last two contests, and as the archdeacon of York he was starting from the same position as the last two bishops. Once the contest had begun, Whitaker could also count on the backing in synod of a majority of the clergy, many of whom were his former students. But Whitaker encountered the same barrier of evangelicals that had handicapped Bishop Bethune and that now constituted a majority of the lay votes in synod. The election quickly turned into one of the most bitter in the fractious history of the Diocese of Toronto; for over a week ballot after ballot failed to break the deadlock. In the end the two sides were forced to agree to a compromise: in return for the evangelicals disbanding their Church Association, which Whitaker described as an *imperium in imperio*, the other side would accept the election of a self-confessed evangelical, the Revd Arthur Sweatman, Rector of New St Paul's, Woodstock, and Archdeacon of Brant in the Diocese of Huron.[10]

The election of Sweatman, a very talented and effective prelate, reduced for a season at least the tensions that had racked the Diocese of Toronto; but the price of peace was the departure of George Whitaker. Having been denied episcopal office for a third time, he resolved to return to England. On 23 September 1879 he announced his resignation to the college council, although council had been aware of his intentions three months before. He sold his family plot in St James' Cemetery and left Toronto in June 1881, having accepted the parish of Newton Tony in his native Wiltshire, a living in the gift of his old college in Cambridge. There he died at the age of seventy, on 28 August 1882.[11]

Finding a replacement for Whitaker proved to be no easy task. The position was first offered to Provost Whitaker's son, Canon George Whitaker, who had excelled in classics at Cambridge and was at that time engaged on a project for the bishop of Truro. The younger Whitaker declined the offer, and the selection of a provost was then caught up in delicate negotiations, led by the new bishop of Toronto, to bring about the amalgamation of Trinity and Wycliffe. When these failed amid much recrimination on both sides, the council turned to a succession of "friends," including Canon Whitaker, who were entrusted with the task of finding a successor in England. These attempts also failed, and so with time running short, in the spring of 1881 a final appeal was made to the bishops of Toronto and Ontario to go to England "with as little delay as possible." Almost at that last minute, on 13 July 1881, it was announced that the Revd Charles William Edmund Body, MA, of St John's College, Cambridge, had accepted the office.[12]

Charles Body came to Trinity along much the same path that had brought George Whitaker to the college some thirty years before. The college had again looked to England for a clergyman and found another young man from Cambridge. Whitaker was forty when he came to Trinity; Body was ten years younger. But the Cambridge that Body knew was very different from the Cambridge that Whitaker had used as a model for so much of Trinity College. His Cambridge had been a church institution with a narrow curriculum that was closed to dissenters and dominated by clerics who saw their positions in the university as an integral part of their careers in the church. But Body's Cambridge, though

Anglican in ethos, had opened its doors to new ideas and new social groups. It had admitted dissenters, expanded its curriculum, and begun to professionalize the position of the university professor, thereby breaking apart what had been central to Whitaker's experience, that is, the integration of a college fellowship and a career in the church. As a result of these changes the prestige of the university and its place in British society had grown enormously.[13]

Even as Whitaker was preparing to take his leave, the council had begun to tackle the serious problems facing Trinity. One strategy was to seek some form of federation with its old rival, the University of Toronto (perhaps explaining why Whitaker had attacked this idea so strongly in his last sermon). Federation had in fact been considered as early as 1868, when the council, in the midst of a financial crisis, set up a committee "to consider the question of affiliation with the Provincial University on such equitable terms as may be agreed upon." This strategy offered a number of advantages. It would quickly solve Trinity's persistent financial woes by giving the college access to the university endowment as well as any new funding the Province of Ontario might bestow. It would give Trinity students a broader range of courses and programmes from which to choose, especially in the sciences, which were very popular and enormously expensive to teach. It might also stymie the rapid progress of Wycliffe College, which was anxious to affiliate with the provincial university. In effect, by linking itself to the University of Toronto, Trinity would be able to offer Anglicans their own college within the provincial university, and would relegate Wycliffe, a purely theological institution, to a much more marginal position. Another strategy was to reject federation, remain independent, and undertake a series of reforms that would, in effect, allow Trinity to compete more successfully with the University of Toronto.

At his first meeting of council, Body made it clear that he would follow the second of these strategies, and he quickly began to introduce measures that would dismantle Whitaker's world and take the college in a bold new direction. The first pillar of the old regime that Body pulled down was the narrow college curriculum. As chair of the curriculum committee he recommended that "it is most desirable at the present time to improve and strengthen the Professional Staff of the College by the appointment of two additional Professors."[14] One of these was to be in divinity, the other in natural science. At the same meeting, council also agreed to set up a special committee, chaired by the provost, to consider ways of "raising an endowment to meet the expense of the two new Professors."[15] When this special committee reported to the next meeting, the direction of Body's plans had become much clearer. The committee proposed that the college undertake a fundraising campaign to raise $100,000 to support the new professorships, erect a chapel, and make major renovations to the existing buildings.

A few months later the curriculum committee called for a further expansion of the curriculum and teaching staff, arguing that it was "essential at as early a date as possible to found chairs in English and English Literature, in Modern Languages, in Moral and Mental Philosophy, and in History."[16] These were very popular subjects that the college hoped would attract new students. To help teach all these new subjects, Body also instituted a programme of teaching fellowships that could be held "for a limited period by graduates of marked intellectual ability."[17]

The academic world that Whitaker had defended so assiduously had crumpled within a year of his departure. Where there had once been a single course of study with a few options around the edges, now students could choose from new "boards of study" that not only encompassed the old subjects – divinity, classics, and mathematics – but also a range of subjects in the sciences and the liberal arts. Plans were also being drawn up to add the buildings and the staff that would be needed to meet the increase in enrolments these reforms were intended to attract.

Provost Body and the council also took steps to discard immediately another founding doctrine of Trinity College – the religious tests that still figured very prominently in the life of the college. Body rejected religious tests in their entirety, replacing them with a simple declaration that "the University confers no Degree whatever, unless the candidate, being a British Subject, has previously signed a declaration of allegiance to Her Majesty the Queen."[18] No longer were dissenters damned; at least those who were loyal to the Crown could now enter the college and take a degree on the same terms as any one else. This important change necessitated an interesting revision to the official history of the college. During Whitaker's tenure the calendars had referred to Strachan's determination to erect a college "for the instruction of the members of the Church of England."[19] The revised calendars, however, imply that the bishop must have had a change of heart after his death, for the official history now stated that it had been the founder's desire to create a college "under the control of the Church of England but open to members of other religious bodies, in which secular instruction should not be dissociated from religious teaching."[20]

The other major effort to expand the size and character of the student body was the new provost's determination to open the doors of Trinity College to women. Here, however, he had to move very carefully. No one seems to have objected strongly to the decision to dispense with religious tests, but the climate for women at Trinity was far from warm. A motion, for example, to rehire, for a second year, a Mrs Morrison, who had been engaged "to deliver lectures in Elocution" (for which she had received a stipend of $50 a term and a fee of $1 per student) was passed by council only after the Revd Langtry's amendment to postpone her reappointment "until enquiries shall have been made as to the possibility of acquiring the Services of a male teacher of elocution" was defeated.[21] Nonetheless, by working skilfully with influential lay members of council, notably the Henderson family, and controlling the composition of certain committees, Body was able to overcome opposition, and within five years of his arrival women joined the men of college with at least the promise of academic equality.[22] Certainly the history of the admitting of women was far less fractious at Trinity than at the University of Toronto.[23]

Body was also very concerned with external relations. Many attacks on the college had come from the outside; even erstwhile friends of the college were critical of its isolated position in society and the church. The provost took steps to draw more support from the graduates of the college and improve relations between the college and the church. He revived convocation and cultivated a close relationship with the new bishop of Toronto. He also revised the composition of the college council to allow for new members to be elected by the graduates of the college and appointed by synod. So successful was he in developing better relations with the church that Wycliffe College felt itself increasingly isolated and was soon asking itself questions about the evangelical bishop it had imposed on the diocese.[24]

The effect of these "reforms" were immediate. Undergraduate enrolments doubled in the decade after Whitaker's departure. New buildings were erected in rapid succession – the chapel in 1884, a west wing of residences in 1889, and an east wing of residences and a gymnasium in 1894; and on 4 April 1899 the Countess of Minto laid the cornerstone of the new St Hilda's College. Finances were brought into order, although the shortcomings of the bursar in 1894, which led to a "large deficiency" in the college accounts, once again placed the college in a precarious financial position.[25] The residential life of the college became much more relaxed, and the collegiate culture of the college prospered.[26] In 1887 two members of the Trinity College cricket club were selected to play for Canada, and A.C. Allen, the son of the chancellor, scored a century at Lords.[27] In view of all the changes that had taken place, the Council of Corporation found that the word "college" no longer adequately described what Trinity had become, and on 15 May 1889 the University of Trinity College was renamed Trinity University.[28] Trinity had been born again.

There was, however, an irony about the course Trinity had followed and the success it enjoyed. While the college had rejected federation with the University of Toronto, there were in fact common threads running through the two competing strategies. Both began from the starting point: that the world the founders had created was no longer viable and that there was no future for Trinity in remaining an exclusive and impoverished Anglican enclave. Both were also convinced that, whether or not Trinity affiliated with the provincial university, it must become a modern, more inclusive institution. And as history would prove, the two strategies were not mutually exclusive. The fact that in 1881 Trinity chose to remain a distinct university did not preclude its turning to federation at a later date. Indeed there was a certain cunning in the way history would unfold. To become competitive with the University of Toronto and remain independent, Trinity jettisoned many of the doctrines that had made it such a distinctive institution, but these were the very doctrines that had stood in the way of federation. So, when Trinity took up the cause of federation in earnest twenty years later, the negotiations on academic matters went very smoothly, largely because on these matters there was almost nothing to discuss.[29] Trinity had entered the modern world, although it was not sure where that world would lead.

Notes

CHAPTER ONE

1 Henry Melville, M.D., *The Rise and Progress of Trinity College, Toronto; with a Sketch of the Life of the Lord Bishop of Toronto as Connected with Church Education in Canada* (Toronto: Henry Rowsell, 1852), 119. Dr Melville was a founding member of the Faculty of Medicine and his "history" provides a detailed description of all the ceremonies surrounding the opening of the college, as well as the texts of the most important speeches.

2 Melville, *The Rise and Progress of Trinity College.* For a discussion of the history of King's College, the relationship between King's College and the University of Toronto, and the place of this controversy in the history of higher education in Ontario, see A.B. McKillop, *Matters of Mind: The University in Ontario, 1791–1951* (Toronto: University of Toronto Press, 1994); D.C. Masters, *Protestant Church Colleges in Canada: A History* (Toronto: University of Toronto

Press, 1966); John Moir, *Church and State in Canada West: Three Studies in the Relation of Denominationalism and Nationalism, 1841–1867* (Toronto: University of Toronto Press, 1959); and W. Stewart Wallace, *A History of the University of Toronto, 1827–1927* (Toronto: University of Toronto Press, 1927).

3 Strachan repeated the same phrase in his pastoral letter to the clergy and laity. The letter was then included (with an error in the date) in J. George Hodgins, *Documentary History of Education in Upper Canada* ... (Toronto: L.K. Cameron, 1902), vol. 9, chap. 6, "Pastoral Letter to the Clergy and Laity of the Diocese of Toronto," 92–3.

4 Melville, *The Rise and Progress of Trinity College*. See also Trinity College Archives, "The Opening of Trinity College, Toronto, Thursday, 15th January, 1852." Once again the procession included students and masters from grammar schools.

5 Trinity College Archives, Matriculation Register. The original declaration is attached to the front cover of the register. The difference in age between these two groups becomes even greater when one takes into account that Strachan and Bethune admitted a group of young men to the institute at Cobourg after they had decided to fold the institute into Trinity. Six of the fifteen on the list, for example, were admitted to the Literary Institute at Cobourg in October 1851, only three months before coming to Trinity. Two other students signed the register later that month, bringing the total of the first class to twenty-one. Since all students entering the college at this time were allowed to keep Michaelmas as a "grace" term, they could graduate by the spring of 1854.

6 Melville, *The Rise and Progress of Trinity College*, 150–1. Bishop Strachan is deservedly honoured as the founder of Trinity College, although the title was largely self-conferred. Nonetheless, Bethune and Whitaker deserve to share in this honour, the former as the head of the seminary that gave birth to Trinity, the latter as the college's

first (and longest-serving, provost. The careers of the two men were also intertwined, a fact that must have occasioned considerable tension. Whitaker succeeded Bethune both as professor of divinity and archdeacon of York; he later ran unsuccessfully against Bethune in the election to succeed Strachan as bishop of Toronto, and suffered a devastating defeat when he failed to become bishop on Bethune's death – a defeat that led to his rapid departure from Trinity College and Canada. Provost Whitaker is discussed in chapter 2. For an account of Bethune's career see Arthur N. Thompson, "Alexander Neil Bethune," *Dictionary of Canadian Biography* (Toronto: University of Toronto Press, 1972), 10: 53–7.

7 "Wherever liberty of thought and expression ... ventured to lift its head, there bludgeon in hand, stood the great Protestant Pope, ready and eager to strike." Dent was one of the true founders of the "liberal" interpretation of Canadian history, and his image of Strachan dominated Canadian historiography for close to a century. John Charles Dent, *The Story of the Upper Canadian Rebellion: Largely derived from Original Sources and Documents* (Toronto: C.B. Robinson, 1885), 23. See also W.L. Morton, "Review Essay: Strachan in the Round," *Journal of Canadian Studies* 4 (November 1969): 46–50.

8 For the most balanced treatment of the life of Bishop Strachan see G.M. Craig, "John Strachan," *Dictionary of Canadian Biography* (Toronto: University of Toronto Press, 1976), 9: 751–66. See also A.N. Bethune, *Memoir of the Right Reverend John Strachan, DD, LLD, first bishop of Toronto* (Toronto and London, 1870); J.L.H. Henderson, "John Strachan as Bishop, 1839–1867" DD thesis, General Synod of Canada, Anglican Church of Canada, 1955); and J.L.H. Henderson, *John Strachan, 1778–1867* (Toronto: University of Toronto Press, 1969).

9 J. George Hodgins lists thirteen university bills introduced into the legislature that failed to pass between 1835 and 1851, seven of these

between the opening of King's College and the founding of the University of Toronto. J. George Hodgins, *Historical and other Papers and Documents Illustrative of the Educational System of Ontario, 1792–1853* (Toronto: L.K. Cameron, 1911), 1: 223–4. See also Moir, *Church and State in Canada West*, and especially McKillop, *Matters of Mind: The University in Ontario*, which does a masterful job of setting this question in its proper religious, social, and economic context (and doing it in fewer than twenty-five pages).

10 Strachan used the same date and founding story when he appealed for financial support in Britain. Trinity College Archives, *Upper Canada, Church University Fund*; Minute Book of Corporation, 4 January 1851; and Trinity College Calendar for 1858. Melville, *The Rise and Progress of Trinity College*; and T.A. Reed, *A History of the University of Trinity College, Toronto 1852–1952* (Toronto: University of Toronto Press, 1952).

11 Brian McKillop uses the phrase "it [Trinity College] was King's College by another name." McKillop, *Matters of Mind: The University in Ontario*, 21.

12 The fact that King's was linked to the Anglican Church did not make it any less a part of the state system, for the church at that time saw itself as a public institution allied to the state.

13 The preparation of candidates for ordination marks an important difference: both King's and Trinity prepared candidates for ordination, but the University of Toronto did not. Consequently, Strachan was able to retrieve from the University of Toronto the theological library that King's College had received from the Society for Promoting Christian Knowledge. The collection, which had been chosen by Strachan, consists of some 400 volumes, each inscribed, "The gift of the Society for Promoting Christian Knowledge to the University of Upper Canada, 1828." The collection is preserved in the Graham Library of Trinity College; it is the earliest accession in any University of Toronto library.

14 J.L.H. Henderson, "The Abominable Incubus: The Church as by Law Established," *Journal of the Canadian Church Historical Society* 11 (1969): 58–66. For a detailed discussion of this issue see William Westfall, *Two Worlds: The Protestant Culture of Nineteenth Century Ontario* (Montreal and Kingston: McGill-Queen's University Press, 1989), especially chapter 4; and William Westfall, "Constructing Public Religions at Private Sites: The Anglican Church in the Shadow of Disestablishment," in Marguerite Van Die, ed., *Religion and Public Life in Canada: Historical and Comparative Perspectives* (Toronto: University of Toronto Press, 2001), 23–49.

15 The two texts that set out the terms of this alliance – William Warburton, *The Alliance Between Church and State; or, The Necessity and Equity of an Established Religion and Test Law Demonstrated* (1736), and William Paley, *The Principles of Moral and Political Philosophy* (1785) – were included in the theological library given to King's College. Warburton's treatise on church and state is one of the few books in this collection that has had to be rebound.

16 Society for the Propagation of the Gospel Archives, C/Canada/Toronto, folio 524 (Rev. C.B. Gribble), 1 April 1842.

17 John Strachan, *A Sermon Preached at York, Upper Canada, Third of July 1825, on the Death of the Late Lord Bishop of Quebec* (Kingston: Macfarlane, 1826).

18 As quoted in Donald Shurman, *A Bishop and His People: John Travers Lewis and the Anglican Diocese of Ontario, 1862–1902* (Kingston: Ontario Diocesan Synod, 1991), 64.

19 Robert L. Fraser, "Like Eden in Her Summer Dress: Gentry, Economy, and Society: Upper Canada, 1812–1840" (PhD thesis, University of Toronto, 1979).

20 "It rested on a more liberal basis than any similar institution in Europe or America." J. George Hodgins expresses great sympathy for Strachan on this matter. Hodgins, *Historical and Other Papers and Documents* 1: 214, 217.

21 Strachan's explanation of chapel services at King's expresses succinctly how he saw the place of the church in King's College: "Parents felt a confidence in its religious character, and, as none, but students belonging to the Church of England, were expected to attend the Chapel morning and evening, sober-minded Dissenters were not offended." In effect, the existence of chapel services reassured everyone that religion was an important part of college life (a point on which all members of the Christian community of Canada West would have agreed): the fact however that non-Anglicans did not have to attend these services meant that dissenters would not be offended by the Anglican presence and consequently could support the college. See J. George Hodgins, *Documentary History of Education in Upper Canada* ... (Toronto: L.K. Cameron, 1902), 9, chap. 5, "History of King's College from 1797 to 1850."

22 In addition to the material cited in note 2, see J.D. Purdy, "John Strachan's Educational Policies," *Ontario History* 64 (March 1972): 45–54; J.D. Purdy, "John Strachan and Education in Canada, 1800–1851" (PhD thesis, University of Toronto, 1962); and Douglas Richardson with J.M.S. Careless, G.M. Craig, and Peter Heyworth, *A Not Unsightly Building: University College and Its History* (Oakville: Mosaic Press for University College, 1990). Professor Richardson's book is especially valuable in this respect for its treatment of the period when King's College occupied the old parliament buildings.

23 Hodgins, *Documentary History of Education*, 9, chap. 6, "Letter to the Secretary of the Society for Promoting Christian Knowledge," 9 May 1850.

24 Trinity College Archives, Minute Book of Corporation, 4 January 1851.

25 Trinity College Archives, Statutes of Trinity College (1852).

26 Hodgins, *Documentary History of Education*, 9, chap. 2, "An Act

to Remove Certain Doubts ...," 49–52. The Act was passed on 10 August 1850.

27 At the University of Toronto, metaphysics, ethics, natural theology, and the evidences of Christianity were "the only subjects which the student was required to study in each of his four years." A.B. McKillop, *Disciplined Intelligence: Critical Inquiry and Canadian Thought in the Victorian Era* (Montreal and Kingston: McGill-Queen's University Press, 1979), 63.

28 In the Strachan papers are two "letters testimonial" for Beaven (in effect two versions of the same letter). These strongly suggest that Strachan wanted to get him out of the University of Toronto. Ontario Archives, Strachan Letter Book, 1852–66, "Letter Testimonial Revd James Beaven, DD," written 1852, revised 1858. T.R. Millman, "James Beaven," *Dictionary of Canadian Biography* (Toronto: University of Toronto Press, 1972), 10: 39–40; and John Campbell, "The Reverend Professor James Beaven, DD, MA," *University of Toronto Monthly* 3 (December 1902): 69–72.

29 G.M. Craig, "John McCaul," *Dictionary of Canadian Biography* (Toronto: University of Toronto Press, 1982), 11: 540–42; and Richardson, *A Not Unsightly Building.*

30 Strachan was also well aware that one of the models for the new Toronto University was the University of London, where an Anglican college (King's) was grafted onto a secular institution. "... being desirous to make it [King's] like the London University or Sir Robert Peel's Irish Colleges." Society for the Propagation of the Gospel Archives, Copies of Letters Received, 177, Toronto Letters Rec'd, 1 (K31), Strachan to SPG, 23 March 1847, 317–21.

31 Moir, *Church and State in Canada West*; Richardson, *A Not Unsightly Building*, especially chap. 1; and McKillop, *Matters of Mind.*

32 For this analysis of the site, especially in relation to the evolution of the city, I am deeply indebted to the scholarship of Mr Stephen A.

Otto, whose detailed knowledge of the history of Toronto, and especially its physical fabric, is remarkable. For more details on these buildings, see Eric Arthur, *Toronto No Mean City*, 3rd ed., revised by Stephen A. Otto (Toronto: University of Toronto Press, 1986). For a contemporary map of the city see *Topographical Plan of the City of Toronto in the Province of Canada, Drawn and Compiled by Sandford A. Fleming*.

33 The college purchased the south part of lot no. 22. The Revd Henry Scadding conducts the reader on a delightful tour of this part of the town in chapter 11 of his *Toronto of Old*, recalling as he and the reader walk from College Avenue (now University Avenue) to the Humber River all the important families who had built their houses along Queen Street. See Henry Scadding, *Toronto of Old: Collections and Recollections Illustrative of the Early Settlement and Social Life of the Capital of Ontario* (Toronto: Adam, Stevenson, 1873), abridged and edited by F.H. Armstrong (Toronto: Oxford University Press, 1966), 238–73. See also Edith G. Firth, ed., *The Town of York, 1793–1815: A Collection of Documents of Early Toronto* and *The Town of York, 1815–1834: A Further Collection of Documents of Early Toronto* (Toronto: Champlain Society, 1962, 1966).

34 Melville, *The Rise and Progress of Trinity College*, 134.

35 Scadding, *Toronto of Old*, 261. Melville described the site as "exceeding beautiful; and the building when finished, will present a striking and pleasing object to vessels approaching or leaving the harbor, which it will, in great measure, overlook." Melville, *The Rise and Progress of Trinity College*, 110.

36 The West Toronto Brewery burned down in 1878 and was rebuilt by Smith and Gemmell. Like most breweries it went through a number of changes, becoming part of the Dominion Brewery in 1936 and the O'Keefe and Carling Breweries in 1946. The building, which survived the college, was demolished in 1961.

37 Trinity College Archives, Invoices, 1876, 1877. For many years the Cosgrave brewery (and other breweries in the west end) invoiced the college by the month for the ale delivered and credited the college with the value of the empty kegs that were returned in working order.

38 A residue of this blessing may perhaps be found in an old college song (recited to the author by the present chancellor, the Rt Revd John C. Bothwell). The provost referred to is F.H. Cosgrave (1926–45): "Behold our genial provost from Ireland, the dear/ It seems his mother named him for a certain brand of beer/ His manner is most gracious but his study is a mess/ And his conversation simply, 'yes, yes, yes, yes, yes, yes ... yes.'"

39 For a good detailed representation of what this part of the city had become, see *The Mapping of Victorian Toronto: The 1884 and 1890 Atlases of Toronto in Comparative Rendition, Charles Edward Goad* (Sutton West, Ont.: Paget Press, 1984), especially plate 21. William Cooke points out that one of the sites considered (and rejected) for the new cathedral was near Trinity College. William G. Cooke, "The Diocese of Toronto and Its Two Cathedrals," *Journal of the Canadian Church Historical Society* 27 (October 1985): 98–115.

40 Firth, *The Town of York*, xxxvi. The map of York prepared by the Royal Engineers in 1833 showing the military reserve is reproduced in Firth, *The Town of York, 1815–34*, facing page 20.

41 Stephen A. Otto, "Note on the Garrison Reserve and Garrison Common," unpublished paper written for the Friends of Fort York, 7 December 1995. "Plan of the Proposed Improvements on Part of the Ordnance Reserve, Toronto," in R. Louis Gentilcore and C. Grant Head, *Ontario History in Maps* (Toronto: Ontario Historical Studies Series 1984), map 7.59.

42 The banner has been restored and returned to the front hall of the college.

43 Trinity College Archives, Minute Book of Corporation, 17 April
   1851. The resolution for grammar schools to "be received into
   Union with the College" was passed on 20 February 1851. The first
   schools to apply were the Church Grammar School in Yorkville
   (renamed the St Paul's Church Grammar School) and the Church
   Grammar School in Cobourg (St Peter's).

44 R.D. Gidney and W.P.J. Millar, *Inventing Secondary Education: The
   Rise of the High School in Nineteenth-Century Ontario* (Montreal
   and Kingston: McGill-Queen's University Press, 1990), especially
   chap. 5.

45 Trinity College Archives, Minute Book of Corporation, 20 February
   1851. It was assumed the headmaster would be a clergyman.

46 The Anglican Church did not entirely give up the fight for a presence in the state-supported system of schooling. The Synod of the
   Diocese of Toronto, at almost every meeting, passed resolutions
   appealing for state support for Anglican common schools, in effect
   claiming the right that Roman Catholics had acquired to have their
   own confessional schools. The church was still trying to make a
   claim that within the evolving system of public education there
   could be both non-denominational and denominational schools.
   The government, however, refused these appeals. *Canons, By-Laws
   and Resolutions Adopted by the Synod of the Diocese of Toronto,
   with an Historical Digest of the Proceedings, from 1851 to 1872
   Inclusive with an Analytical Index of the Whole* (Toronto: Leader
   Office, 1873), 207–17.

47 R.D. Gidney and W.P.J. Millar, *Inventing Secondary Education: The
   Rise of the High School in Nineteenth-Century Ontario* (Montreal
   and Kingston: McGill-Queen's University Press, 1990).

48 Trinity College Archives, Minute Book of Corporation, 10 January
   1883, 20 June 1883, 13 February 1884, 10 March 1886.

49 The calendar of Trinity College School was then published as an
   addendum to the calendar of Trinity College.

50 Trinity College Archives, Minute Book of Corporation, 7 November 1850. Melville, *The Rise and Progress of Trinity College*, 104ff.

51 George W. Spragge, "Trinity Medical College," *Ontario History* (June, 1966): 63–98.

52 "Lawyers must, from the very nature of our political institutions, from there being no great land-proprietors, no privileged orders, become the most powerful profession, and must in time possess more influence and authority than any other." John Strachan, *An Appeal to the Friends of Religion and Literature in Behalf of the University of Upper Canada* (London: R. Gilbert, 1827), 8.

53 R.D. Gidney and W.P.J. Millar, *Professional Gentlemen: The Professions in Nineteenth-Century Ontario* (Toronto: University of Toronto Press, 1994).

54 This fact has largely escaped the growing literature on state formation in Canada. See Alan Greer and Ian Radforth, eds, *Colonial Leviathan: State Formation in Mid-Nineteenth Century Ontario* (Toronto: University of Toronto Press, 1994); and Westfall, "The Anglican Church in the Shadow of Disestablishment," in Van Die, ed., *Religion and Public Life in Canada*.

55 Trinity College Archives, Minute Book of Corporation. On 10 May 1871, the corporation changed the statutes to allow students to petition the chancellor or vice chancellor to dispense with the offending declaration. At the same time the corporation was given the power, if it saw "good cause," to allow "any Professor or Professors of the Faculty of Medicine, to dispense with the above mentioned qualification and subscriptions." See also Spragge, "Trinity Medical College," *Ontario History* (June, 1966): 63–98. Enrolments in medicine were critically important to the college, and when the medical faculty was dissolved in 1856 the financial health of the college (which was always precarious) was put in grave danger. When the faculty returned in 1872, enrolments grew rapidly, quickly outpacing those in arts and divinity.

56 He also found himself in hot water for the same reason. John Strachan, *An Appeal to the Friends of Religion and Literature in Behalf
of the University of Upper Canada* (London: R. Gilbert, 1827).

57 The Revd Thomas Dowell Phillipps (BA 1855) began his preparation
for the church at Cobourg and was the eleventh student to sign the
matriculation register. He was an outstanding cricketer, a genuine
all-rounder, one of the very best the college has produced. He was
also a generous soul, giving a bat for the best score in a college
match.

58 "Till a Divinity School is established in connexion with King's College or the Cathedral." Ontario Archives, Strachan Letter Book,
1839–43, "Letter to Joseph R. Thompson," 4 November 1841, and
"Letter to Alex Menzies," 5 November 1841.

59 Unfortunately a rival group of faculty members that controlled academic affairs at St Andrew's would not grant Strachan's request. He
then turned to King's College, Aberdeen, which awarded Bethune its
doctorate in 1847. Ontario Archives, Strachan Letter Book, 1844–9,
"Letter to Rev. Thomas Duncan," 9 November 1845, and "Letter to
Rev. Principal Jack, DD," 22 January 1847.

60 Ontario Archives, Strachan Letter Book, 1844–9, Letter (salutation
not specified) 29 June 1847. He had also considered the name
"Percy College."

61 "During the whole period of its continuance, that is from January,
1842, to January, 1852, when Trinity College was established, seven-
ty-seven students in all attended, of whom sixty-nine have been
ordained, who are thus distributed: one in the West Indies, two in
England, four in Lower Canada, and sixty-two in this diocese. In
January, 1852, fifteen pupils were transferred from the institution at
Cobourg to Trinity College, Toronto, and are included in the sixty-
two above mentioned. Among those ordained are several of the most
useful and zealous clergymen now labouring in the diocese, and I
believe they look back with interest and affection to the place in

which they received their instruction and preparation for holy orders." *Proceedings of the Synod of the United Church of England and Ireland, of the Diocese of Toronto* ... (Toronto: Rowsell and Ellis, 1861), 243-4.

62 Trinity College Archives, Degree Book. For the convocation of 19 December 1861 the Degree Book lists ten "former students of the late Theological College at Cobourg" for the degree of BA and another former student for the MA. For the convocation of 18 December 1862, there are two for the BA and seven for the MA. These were granted in accordance with "the terms of an order of the Corporation passed October 1855."

63 For material on Britain see Alan Haig, *The Victorian Clergy* (Sydney: Croom Helm, 1984); M.A. Crowther, *Church Embattled: Religious Controversy in Mid-Victorian England* (Newton Abbot: David and Charles, 1970); F.W. Bullock, *A History of Training for the Ministry of the Church of England and Wales from 1800 to 1874* (St Leonards-On-Sea: Budd and Gillat, 1955); and David A. Dowland, *Nineteenth-Century Anglican Theological Training: The Redbrick Challenge* (Oxford: Clarendon Press, 1997).

64 Trinity College Archives, Minute Book of Corporation, 23 January 1851. For a view and description of St Aidan's, see *The Builder*, 8 no. 374 (6 April 1850): 162-3.

65 Melville, *The Rise and Progress of Trinity College*, 156. For an analysis of such architectural appreciations see George L. Hersey, *High Victorian Gothic: A Study in Associationism* (Baltimore, Md: John Hopkins University Press, 1972); and James F. White, *The Cambridge Movement: The Ecclesiologists and the Gothic Revival* (Cambridge: Cambridge University Press, 1962).

66 Trinity College Archives, "Minutes of the Proceedings at the Visitation of the Lord Bishop of Toronto Held in the Church of the Holy Trinity, Toronto, on the 1st & 2nd May, 1851," *A Charge Delivered to the Clergy of the Diocese of Toronto in May* MDCCCLI *by John,*

Lord Bishop of Toronto (Toronto: Diocesan Press, 1851), 51ff.

67 See Westfall, *Two Worlds*, especially 112–15; and T.R. Millman, "Beginnings of the Synodical Movement in Colonial Anglican Churches with Special Reference to Canada," *Journal of the Canadian Church Historical Society* 21 (1979): 3–19.

68 Hodgins, *Documentary History of Education*, 4, chap. 14, "The University Building Commenced – Laying of the Corner Stone."

CHAPTER TWO

1 Ontario Archives, Strachan Papers, Letter Book to the Societies, 1839–1866.

2 John Strachan, *An Appeal to the Friends of Religion and Literature, in Behalf of the University of Upper Canada* (London: R. Gilbert, 1827), 20–1.

3 John Moir, *Church and State in Canada West: Three Studies in the Relation of Denominationalism and Nationalism, 1841–1867* (Toronto: University of Toronto Press, 1959), 76; John Moir, "The Settlement of the Clergy Reserves, 1840–1855," *Canadian Historical Review* 37 (March 1956): 26–62; and William Westfall, "The Doctrine of Expediency: Lord Durham's Report and the Alliance of Church and State," *Journal of Canadian Studies* 25, no. 1 (Spring 1990): 178–90.

4 Society for the Propagation of the Gospel Archives, D Series, D14, "A Letter to the Right Honourable Lord John Russell, etc. On the Present State of the Church in Canada by the Bishop of Toronto," 20 February 1851.

5 See William Westfall, *Two Worlds: The Protestant Culture of Nineteenth-Century Ontario* (Montreal and Kingston: McGill-Queen's University Press, 1989), especially chap. 4.

6 Ontario Archives, Strachan Papers, Draft of Letter [from] John Beverley Robinson to the Hon Inspector General, 7 September 1852.

7 "Pastoral Letter to the Clergy and Laity of the Diocese of Toronto," as quoted in Henry Melville, MD, *The Rise and Progress of Trinity College, Toronto; with a Sketch of the Life of the Lord Bishop of Toronto as Connected with Church Education in Canada* (Toronto: Henry Rowsell, 1852), 93.

8 "The plans of the proposed college to be called St Aiden's [*sic*] College" were given to the architects on 23 January 1851. On 30 January, Kivas Tully asked for more time to prepare his drawings. Trinity College Archives, Minute Book of Corporation, 23 January 1851, 30 January 1851.

9 Most notably, St Hilda's College did not move into its own building until 1899, eleven years after the decision was made to found a college for women. In the interval women had to occupy temporary accommodations near the campus. The same thing happened when St Hilda's moved to Hoskin Avenue. T.A. Reed, *A History of Trinity College Toronto, 1852–1952* (Toronto: University of Toronto Press, 1952), especially chap. 9.

10 Trinity College Archives, Minute Book of Corporation, 10 and 15 April 1850.

11 Ibid., 4 January 1851. The importance of this meeting was marked by copying the official version of the founding of Trinity College into the Minute Book of Corporation. The relationship between the Church University Board and the Provisional Council is not clear. The council was set up at a meeting of the board and drew its members from the larger board. The Church University Board, however, continued to meet, and it marched separately from the council in the procession on 30 April 1851. Acting on the power granted by the provincial Act of incorporation, Strachan on 17 September 1851 transformed the Provisional Council (with very few changes in membership) into the Council of Trinity College or, to use its official name, the Council of the Corporation of Trinity College.

12 Ibid., 4 January 1851.

13 Ibid., 16 January 1851. The bishop also cast the deciding vote in the event of a tie.

14 Ibid., 23 January 1851. The currency here is "provincial currency," which was worth about 15 per cent less than the British pound sterling. Unfortunately, the records do not differentiate clearly between the two currencies. The college accounts were kept in provincial currency, and it is reasonably safe to assume that all amounts given here except the gifts received from Britain, are in provincial currency.

15 Ibid., 14 March 1851, 17 March 1851. Professor Douglas Richardson has pointed out how Cumberland and Storm borrowed the mansard roofs from the St Aidan's plan for their design for University College. Kivas Tully replaced these roofs with lanterns in his winning design for Trinity College. Douglas Richardson with J.M.S. Careless, G.M. Craig and Peter Heyworth, *A Not Unsightly Building: University College and Its History* (Oakville: Mosaic Press for University College, 1990), 76.

16 For a more detailed architectural analysis of the college, see Graham Warwick Owen, "Projects for Trinity College Toronto," *The Journal of Canadian Art History* 4 (Spring 1977): 61–72.

17 Henry Melville, MD, *The Rise and Progress of Trinity College, Toronto; with a Sketch of the Life of the Lord Bishop of Toronto as Connected with Church Education in Canada* (Toronto: Henry Rowsell, 1852), 156–60.

18 The gates themselves were given to Trinity College School in Port Hope. The St Hilda's College building, designed by Eden Smith, also survives. It was built in 1899 near the northwest corner of the property. It faced to the south and overlooked the Gore Vale ravine.

19 Scadding refers to the "elmy dale which gives such agreeable variety to the park of Trinity College." Henry Scadding, *Toronto of Old: Collections and Recollections Illustrative of the Early Settlement and Social Life of the Capital of Ontario* (Toronto: Adam, Stevenson,

1873), abridged and edited by F.H. Armstrong (Toronto: Oxford University Press, 1966), 261.

20 For Strachan's account of the building and the importance of residential life, see his speeches in Melville, *The Rise and Progress of Trinity College*, 134.

21 SPG Archives, C/Canada/ Toronto, Folio 518 (John Strachan), "The Present State of Trinity College," Strachan to SPG, 15 March 1852. Melville, *The Rise and Progress of Trinity College*, 157.

22 Trinity College Archives, Minute Book of Corporation, 9 March 1852, 18 March 1852, 27 May 1852, 3 June 1852. On 9 March 1852 it was also announced that the contractors had failed. T.A. Reed, *A History of the University of Trinity College, 1852–1952* (Toronto: University of Toronto Press, 1952), 51.

23 "The Council having been taken by surprise by the amount of the extra work." Trinity College Archives, Minute Book of Corporation, 1 March 1852.

24 Trinity College Archives, "Trinity College, Toronto, 6th December 1859."

25 It should be pointed out that the endowment was seen by the government as an alternative to direct government grants. F.A. Mouré, "Outline of the Financial History of the University," *The University of Toronto and Its Colleges, 1827–1906* (Toronto: University Library, 1906), 71–7.

26 Ontario Archives, Strachan Papers, "Memorandum of a Scheme for establishing a Church University in Upper Canada To Be Endowed From Private Sources Only," 29 May 1850.

27 SPG Archives, D Series, D 14, "Pastoral Letter to the Clergy and Laity of the Diocese of Toronto," 7 February 1850.

28 Trinity College Archives, Minute Book of Corporation, 20 October 1852 and 26 May 1853.

29 Ontario Archives, Strachan Papers, "Appeal for Subscriptions in England for Trinity College," no date. "The success which had

attended the effort to erect the College was, in a great degree owing to the fact that Dr Burnside had placed his name for so large a sum at the head of the Subscription List." Trinity College Archives, Minute Book of Corporation, 9 April 1853.

30 Trinity College Archives, Minute Book of Corporation, 18 April 1850.

31 Ibid., "Early Benefactors of Trinity College." Melville includes a slightly different list of benefactors as the final appendix of his book.

32 Ibid., Minute Book of Corporation, 22 April 1852.

33 "For although the positive payments have been nothing great, we have many promises." Ontario Archives, Strachan Papers, Bethune to Strachan, 1 September 1852 and 19 November 1852.

34 In 1998 the fund established by this gift had a capital value of $11,716. The lands the SPG gave to the college were sold in 1855 for £9,155. Trinity College Archives, Minute Book of Corporation, 16 June 1855.

35 SPG Archives, Copies of Letters Sent, Toronto, E.R. Fayerman to Strachan, 24 September 1851, and Hawkins to Strachan, 7 May 1852. Trinity College Archives, Minute Book of Corporation, 20 November 1852. Melville states that Oxford University gave £500. Melville, *The Rise and Progress of Trinity College*, 132–3.

36 Strachan reviewed the amounts raised in his opening address at the inauguration. The meagreness of the English donations were an embarrassment because of the number of times Strachan seemed prepared to defer to what he believed to be the views of these donors. He mentions by name Charles Hampton Turner, Esq. FRS, Rooks Nest Park, Surrey, who gave £500. Melville, *The Rise and Progress of Trinity College*, 133.

37 Ontario Archives, Strachan Papers, Report of Trinity College for the Academical Year 1852–3. In part the American campaign was based upon the hope that Trinity could draw British students from the United States and the West Indies who wanted to be educated in an

English environment but could not afford to go to Britain.

38 Trinity College Archives, Minute Book of Corporation, 16 September 1852, 30 December 1852, 13 January 1853, and 12 May 1853. Trinity Church, New York, donated $1,000 to the college out of a special collection from its Jubilee Service in 1852. Minute Book of Corporation, 1 October 1852. Richard Ruggle, "William McMurray," *Dictionary of Canadian Biography* (Toronto: University of Toronto Press, 1990), 12: 680–2.

39 SPG Archives, C Series, C/Canada/Toronto, Folio 518 (John Strachan), Strachan to SPG, 26 February 1853.

40 Ontario Archives, Strachan Letter Book, 1854–62, Letters to J.H. Cameron, 30 March 1855 and 20 April 1855.

41 Strachan reported a similar figure (£16,465) to the SPG. SPG Archives, C Series, C/Canada/Toronto, Folio 518 (John Strachan), Strachan to SPG, 22 June 1855. See also Diocese of Toronto Archives, Clergy Commutation Fund, Synod of Toronto.

42 "Trinity College, tho self-supporting to some extent, depends at present in great measure on the 1,200 pounds currency allowed us ... from the Clergy Reserve Fund." Ontario Archives, Strachan Letter Book, 1854–62, Letter to the Bishop of Quebec, 21 March 1854. A good account of the negotiations appears in Cameron's report to the council on 30 June 1855. By investing this sum in debentures, the college increased its "permanent capital" by £20,000, which yielded a sum close to the original figure of £1,200. Trinity College Archives, Minute Book of Corporation, 30 June 1855. There was, however, one important casualty in these complex financial dealings. The original agreement with the SPG had specified clearly that a large portion of this grant (some £300 to £400 a year) was to be set aside to support candidates preparing for ordination. But now the entire amount of this grant covered only the salaries of the three new professors. Although it is hard to trace the precise movement of money, it is clear that with the founding of Trinity College the number and the value of

divinity scholarships rapidly declined. Indeed the SPG may well have given the Jubilee Scholarships, not to add to the college scholarships, but to make up for at least a part of this loss. The decline in support clearly affected the number of candidates coming forward to the church, especially in times of financial hardship. The problem became grave enough to be taken up by a special committee of synod in 1859. See *Proceedings of the Synod of the United Church of England and Ireland, in the Diocese of Toronto ... MDCCCLIX* (Toronto: Rowsell and Ellis, 1859).

43 Trinity College Archives, Minute Book of Corporation, 6 November 1851.

44 This figure includes local subscriptions, the money from Britain, the commutation settlement, and the revenue from sale of lands.

45 The costs of scholarships (£345) had been treated as an item with its own endowment; by this point, however, scholarships became simply another item of expenditure.

46 James Talman has pointed out the high percentage of the Anglican clergy who had university degrees. J.J. Talman, "Some Notes on the Clergy of the Church of England in Upper Canada Prior to 1840," *Royal Society of Canada, Papers and Transactions* 2 (1938): 57–66.

47 Reed, *A History of the University of Trinity College*, 46–7.

48 Ontario Archives, Strachan Papers, Letter Book to the Societies, 1839–1866, Strachan to Hawkins, 16 February 1851. Strachan's statistics are both accurate and misleading. The census of 1851 gives the population of Canada West as 952,004, but for reasons of religious faith and sex the vast majority of these inhabitants could not take a degree from Trinity. In 1851, 223,100 inhabitants of Canada West identified themselves as Anglicans, and one presumes a good half of these were women.

49 Ibid., Strachan to Hawkins, 16 February 1851.

50 Success, Strachan declared, came only "after much trouble and many disappointments." Quoted in Melville, *The Rise and Progress*

of Trinity College, 132. The "wardenship" was offered to a Mr
Cowie (the spelling is not clear). SPG Archives, Copies of Letters
Sent, Toronto, vol. 1, Hawkins to Strachan, 26 June 1851. As late as
October 1851 the council in Toronto was led to believe that "Mr
Godd would be appointed Professor of Mathematics." Trinity Col-
lege Archives, Minute Book of Corporation, 9 October 1851.

51 Ontario Archives, Strachan Letter Book, 1854-62, Letter to the
Bishop of Nova Scotia, 12 June 1854.

52 For material on Whitaker see Reed, *A History of the University of
Trinity College,* especially chaps 2, 3, and 4, and Christopher Fergus
Headon, "George Whitaker," *Dictionary of Canadian Biography*
(Toronto: University of Toronto Press, 1982), XI: 916-17. I am also
indebted to the Whitaker materials that my colleague Professor
Thomas McIntire has kindly shared with me. These include biogra-
phical materials, copies of sermons, and an unpublished article, C.T.
McIntire, "The Making of Christian Gentlemen: The Social Message
of Provost George Whitaker in Trinity College, Toronto, 1851-81."

53 Elizabeth Crittall, ed., *A History of Wiltshire* (Oxford: Oxford University Press, 1965), vol. 80. Philip Whitaker owned, either on his
own or with his brother, 76 acres, 4 roods, and 27 perches of land.
Survey of Property enclosed with letter from Mrs Jean Morrison to
Dr T. McIntire, 19 June 1986.

54 The oath of office for the Chancellor of Trinity College was the
same as "the oaths required by the Chancellor of Cambridge." Trinity College Archives, Minute Book of Corporation, 3 March 1853.

55 "As the statute makes the College a Church of England Institution
and has given it a Council with full power ... to prescribe its discipline and regulate the government and manage its property, there
seems nothing more to be desired than that the Crown should
enable the College by Royal Charter to confer degrees." Trinity College Archives, Minute Book of Corporation, 25 March 1852. Strachan believed that granting degrees by Royal Charter, rather than

provincial statute, gave the degrees much wider authority.

56 J. George Hodgins, *Documentary History of Education in Upper Canada* ... (Toronto: L.K. Cameron, 1902), 10, chap. 6, "Correspondence of the Honourable Peter B. de Blaquiere, Chancellor of the University of Toronto, and Bishop Strachan on the Church University," 51–4. To reinforce this misinterpretation the Royal Charter was reproduced prominently in the new college calendar.

57 Trinity College Archives, Minute Book of Corporation, 6, 13, and 27 November 1851; 4 December 1851.

58 Ibid., *Statutes of Trinity College*, 1852. The head of the college was to be styled "the provost of Trinity College," and he "shall be a clergyman, in Holy Orders, of the United Church of England and Ireland." All the other professors (in every faculty) also had to be members of the church and "shall, upon ... admission to office, sign and subscribe the Thirty-nine Articles of religion, as declared and set forth in the Book of Common Prayer, and the three articles of the Thirty-sixth Canon." The statutes are entered into the Minute Book of Corporation on 4 December 1851.

59 Ontario Archives, Strachan Papers, Letter from Whitaker, Parry, and Irving to Bishop Strachan regarding resolution of Trinity College Council, 9 December 1851. Whitaker proposed to divide authority and power by separating "university" matters (such as property, revenue, and degrees) and "college" matters (such as daily academic life and discipline). The former were to be the preserve of the council, while the latter were to be under the exclusive control of the provost and professors, whose decisions could be appealed to a "visitor" from outside the college.

60 Trinity College Archives, Minute Book of Corporation, 11 December 1851, 18 December 1851, 31 December 1851. Sixteen new statutes (and other regulations) were enacted by the council on 3 March 1853. These followed on the granting of the Royal Charter

and dealt entirely with the office of chancellor, convocation, and granting of degrees. They did not change the statutes passed on 31 December 1851.

61 Ibid., *The Calendar of the University of Trinity College, Toronto, for the Year 1853*, 15; *Statutes of Trinity College, Toronto; As Amended by the Corporation on the 8th December 1863* (Toronto: Rowsell and Ellis, 1864). The provision that students must be members of the church to take a degree remained in force until 1871, when it was amended to allow the chancellor to dispense with this requirement "on the ground that the candidate is not a member of the United Church of England and Ireland." This explanation is written into this document in Whitaker's own hand. It was not removed until after Whitaker's departure.

62 Ibid., *Statutes of Trinity College* (1852).

63 "The course of study is shaped as closely as possible after the models of Oxford and Cambridge," SPG Archives, D Series, D Toronto, 1860–7, 706–8.

64 Trinity College Archives, *Calendar of the University of Trinity College* (1866), Subjects for Mathematical Honours.

65 Calendars were indeed calendars, which began with a complete calendar of the year setting out holidays, saint's days (including that of King Charles the Martyr), the college terms and examinations, and the major festivals in the college year.

66 A student writing the matriculation examination "must have entered his sixteenth year." To write the examination for a scholarship "he must have entered his seventeenth year." See, for example, Trinity College Archives, *Calendar of the University of Trinity College* (1875); *Statutes of Trinity College*, Regulations for Students in Arts; and *Calendar of the University of Trinity College* (1863), 33.

67 Trinity College Archives, Minute Book of Corporation, 29 May 1878 and 11 December 1878. See R.D. Gidney and W.P.J. Millar,

Inventing Secondary Education: The Rise of the High School in Nineteenth-Century Ontario (Montreal: McGill-Queen's University Press, 1990).

68 Ibid., *Statutes of Trinity College* (1864), 10–11. See also Reed, *A History of the University of Trinity College*, 52–4.

69 During Whitaker's tenure, this schedule of examinations was revised to conform more closely to the structure of the academic years rather than the course of study as a whole, so that instead of having an examination at the beginning, the middle, and the end of the programme, students wrote the previous examination at the *end* of the second year (a change introduced in 1864) and wrote a *new* examination ("the First Year Examination") at the end of the first year (a change introduced in 1876). At the same time these examinations and the list of required texts were increasingly subdivided by what might now be called discipline (divinity, classics, and mathematics) rather than listed together. All of these changes, however, served to reinforce the basic character of the original college curriculum. Trinity College Archives, *Calendar of the University of Trinity College* (1864, 1876, 1877).

70 The statutes of 1852 repeat almost verbatim the provisional statutes. Trinity College Archives, *Statutes of Trinity College* (1852), Regulations for Theology Students.

71 "Undergraduates of Trinity College who have attended the Lectures of the Arts Course for one year, provided that they have obtained the approval of the provost and Professors, and are of the full age of 21 years." Trinity College Archives, *Statutes of Trinity College* (1864), Regulations for Students in Arts and Divinity. See also *Calendar of the University of Trinity College* (1854).

72 Trinity College Archives, *Calendar of the University of Trinity College* (1865); *Statutes of Trinity College*, Regulations for Students in Arts. In 1860 provision was made for "admitting Candidates to Degrees in Arts, by examination, without residence." This was

restricted to men over twenty-five who provided adequate testimonials and justifications; they were still required to pass all three examinations. This experiment was to run for five years, but in 1864 it was not renewed. *Calendar of the University of Trinity College* (1860, 1865).

73 Trinity College Archives, *University of Trinity College Calendar* (1865).

74 Ibid., *Statutes of Trinity College*, Regulations for Theology Students.

75 SPG Archives, D Series, D Toronto 1860–7, 708.

76 The Revd Francis Richard Tane, for example, signed the matriculation register in October 1852 and was ordained by Strachan in 1854. In 1877 he still remained on the books as an undergraduate.

77 Trinity College Archives, *Calendar of the University of Trinity College* (1857).

78 In 1866 Dr Bovell took over Professor Hind's lectures in chemistry and geology, lecturing in the first year in chemistry, in the second year in "Experimental Philosophy," and in the third year "Natural Theology." He also lectured in "Moral Philosophy" to students in Divinity. His prize – "Dr Bovell's Medal" – was awarded for the best essay in natural theology. When the Medical School was re-established in 1871, he became professor of medicine. Trinity College Archives, *Calendar of the University of Trinity College* (1866, 1871).

79 For an excellent study of Bovell's ideas in relation to the broad contours of critical thought in Victorian Canada, see A.B. McKillop, *A Disciplined Intelligence: Critical Inquiry and Canadian Thought in the Victorian Era* (Montreal: McGill-Queen's University Press, 1979), 59–91.

80 James Bovell, *Outlines of Natural Theology, for the Use of the Canadian Student* (Toronto, 1859), introduction. Bovell also tried to confirm scientifically the biblical account of the order of creation. His book, which was published on the very eve of the Darwinian

revolution, sets out clearly the two critical assumptions – the order of nature was both static and moral – that Charles Darwin would so unsettle.

81 McKillop, *Disciplined Intelligence*, 63.

82 Trinity College Archives, *Provisional Statutes of Trinity College*, Regulations for Students in Arts.

83 Ibid., *Statutes of Trinity College* (1852), Regulations for Students in Arts, Regulations for Theology Students.

84 *Proceedings at the Installation of the Chancellor of Trinity College, Toronto, on Friday, the 3rd day of July, 1853* (Toronto: British Canadian, 1853), 28–9.

85 Ibid., 28.

86 Ontario Archives, Strachan Letter Book, 1854–62, Letter to Revd James Usher, 7 April 1854.

87 Alison Prentice, "Education and the Metaphor of the Family: The Upper Canadian Example," in *Education and Social Change*, ed. Michael B. Katz and Paul H. Mattingly (New York: New York University Press, 1975), 110–32.

88 SPG Archives, Copies of Letters Sent, 123 (Toronto Letters Sent), vol. 1, SPG to John Strachan, 3 February 1847, 98–101. In 1847 the SPG circulated a series of questions to the educational institutions it supported. They imply that the Society was encouraging institutions to establish a strong communal and residential life, asking, for example, if there were residences and whether students and faculty took meals together. For Strachan's response, see SPG Archives, Copies of Letters Received, 177 (Toronto Letters Received), vol. 1, John Strachan to SPG, 23 March 1847, 317–21.

CHAPTER THREE

1 Ontario Archives, Strachan Papers, Letter Book to the Societies, 1839–1866, Strachan to Hawkins, 16 February 1851.

2 Ibid., Whitaker, Parry, and Irving to Bishop Strachan regarding resolution of Trinity College Council, 9 December 1851.

3 As quoted in Henry Melville, MD, *The Rise and Progress of Trinity College, Toronto; with a Sketch of the Life of the Lord Bishop of Toronto as Connected with Church Education in Canada* (Toronto: Henry Roswell, 1852), 120–1.

4 "Yet another fundamental assumption in shaping the structure of Upper Canadian education was that schools were extensions of, and subordinate to, families." R.D. Gidney and W.P.J. Millar, *Inventing Secondary Education: The Rise of the High School in Nineteenth-Century Ontario* (Montreal and Kingston: McGill-Queen's University Press, 1990), 23; and Alison Prentice, "Education and the Metaphor of the Family: The Upper Canadian Example," in *Education and Social Change*, ed. Michael B. Katz and Paul H. Mattingly (New York: New York University Press, 1975), 110–32.

5 John Strachan, "Opening Address at the inauguration of Trinity College, 15 January 1852," Melville, *The Rise and Progress of Trinity College*, 136. The addresses are also reprinted in J. George Hodgins, *Documentary History of Education in Upper Canada ...* (Toronto: L.K. Cameron, 1902), vol. 5, chap. 4, "The Inauguration and the Opening of Trinity College, 1852."

6 Melville, *The Rise and Progress of Trinity College*, 136.

7 *Proceedings at the Installation of the Chancellor of Trinity College, Toronto, on Friday, the 3rd day of July, 1853* (Toronto: British Canadian, 1853), 29. "Returned to that simple and confiding piety which he relished and practiced in his earliest infancy." Ibid., 29.

8 Melville, *The Rise and Progress of Trinity College*, 136–7.

9 Ibid., 136.

10 Ibid.

11 Ibid.

12 *Proceedings at the Installation of the Chancellor of Trinity College*, 29.

13 C.T. McIntire, "The Making of Christian Gentlemen: The Social Message of Provost George Whitaker in Trinity College, Toronto, 1851–81" (unpublished paper).

14 A.B. McKillop's fine book, *A Disciplined Intelligence*, places the need for order and discipline at the intersection of the drive for knowledge (the myth of freedom) and the demands of faith (the myth of concern). A well-disciplined intelligence could advance knowledge and preserve the foundations of faith. At Trinity the metaphor of the family served a similar function for the body, providing the discipline and moral codes in which learning could flourish. A.B. McKillop, *A Disciplined Intelligence: Critical Inquiry and Canadian Thought in the Victorian Era* (Montreal and Kingston: McGill-Queen's University Press, 1979).

15 Melville, *The Rise and Progress of Trinity College*, 136.

16 Ibid., 135–6.

17 Ibid., 133.

18 Ibid., 137.

19 "St John the Baptist, an Exemplar to Christian Ministers," in *A Sermon Preached in the Chapel of Trinity College, Sunday June 14, 1860 by George Whitaker, MA, Provost of Trinity College, published at the request of the professors and students of the College* (Toronto: Henry Rowsell, 1860); and "The Holy Spirit's Sealing," in *Sermons Preached in Toronto for the Most Part in the Chapel of Trinity College by George Whitaker, MA* (London: Rivingtons; Toronto: Willing and Williamson, 1882).

20 Both sides recognized the reality (and power) of such families. Francis Bond Head saw them as a "natural" part of any proper social hierarchy; Mackenzie saw them as artificial and held together only by patronage and self-interest. See Graeme Patterson, "Whiggery, Nationality, and the Upper Canadian Reform Tradition," *Canadian Historical Review*, 56, no. 1 (March 1975): 25–44.

21 A.B. McKillop, *Matters of Mind: The University in Ontario,*

1791–1951 (Toronto: University of Toronto Press, 1994), chap. 1.

22 John Strachan, "Opening Address at the Inauguration of Trinity College, 15 January 1852"; Melville, *The Rise and Progress of Trinity College,* 136.

23 "St John the Baptist," 11; "The Holy Spirit's Sealing," 152.

24 For a discussion of this cultural transformation, see William Westfall, *Two Worlds: The Protestant Culture of Nineteenth Century Ontario* (Montreal and Kingston: McGill-Queen's University Press, 1989).

25 "Our Lord's Choice of the Twelve," in *Sermons Preached in Toronto for the Most Part in the Chapel of Trinity College by George Whitaker,* MA (London: Rivingtons; Toronto: Willing and Williamson, 1882), 11.

26 Jack Wright suggested the popular advertising phrase "BA all the way."

27 A. Gregory Schneider, *The Way of the Cross Leads Home: The Domestication of American Methodism* (Bloomington: Indiana University Press, 1993). See also Phyllis D. Airhart and Margaret Lamberts Bendroth, eds, *Faith Traditions and the Family* (Louisville, Ky.: Westminster John Knox Press, 1996); and Ann Douglas, *The Feminization of American Culture* (New York: Anchor Books, 1988), especially the preface.

28 *Trinity University Review,* 23 June 1902, 121. Paraphrased in T.A. Reed, *A History of Trinity College, Toronto 1852–1952* (Toronto: University of Toronto Press, 1952), 50–1.

29 Bethune was well schooled in this tradition, having been educated in this way by Strachan both as a student in his grammar school and as a candidate for ordination. For a fascinating description of this gentlemanly world, see the account of the choice of a gift to express the students' "gratitude and esteem" to their "Venerable Principal." After a well-conducted and thoughtful discussion they commissioned a portrait of Bethune by Theophile Hamil, which they then presented

to "his Lady and family." This outstanding work of Canadian portraiture found its way to Trinity and now hangs in Seeley Hall. *The Church*, 20 February 1851, 234.

30 SPG Archives, D Series, D Toronto 1860–7, 170.

31 Trinity College Archives, "Trinity College Conducted as a Mere Boys' School, Not as a College," 18. For a rich account of Denison's life see Carl Berger, *The Sense of Power: Studies in the Ideas of Canadian Imperialism, 1867–1914* (Toronto: University of Toronto Press, 1970).

The Minute Book of Corporation reports many instances of students' petitioning the council to change the rules. It also records the punishments meted out to those who had broken the rules. At its meeting on 10 February 1863, for example, the council rejected a memorial from the students, telling them to "give such attention to their studies as will meet the approval of the professors." A petition concerning the wearing of the cap and gown came before Corporation on 11 December 1866, when it was agreed that students could dispense with the cap (but not the gown) "in the streets" during winter. On 9 November 1869 students were allowed to dispense with the cap and gown outside the college between two and six o'clock in the afternoon. Trinity College Archives, Minute Book of Corporation (for the dates indicated).

32 Ontario Archives, Strachan Letter Book, "Notes of last letter to Professor Duncan," 12 April 1858. In comparing himself to Arnold, Strachan pointed out that he had begun earlier, taught longer, and lived longer than Arnold. "Look at the stirring sermons of the late Doctor Arnold of Rugby." He also referred to Dr Moberly (Winchester) and Dr Vaughan (Harrow). See J. George Hodgins, *Documentary History of Education in Upper Canada* ... (Toronto: L.K. Cameron, 1902), vol. 9, chap. 5, "History of King's College from 1797 to 1850." See also J.D. Purdy, "John Strachan and Education in Canada, 1800–1851" (PhD thesis, University of Toronto, 1962).

33 Melville, *The Rise and Progress of Trinity College*, 136.

34 Ibid., 135–6.

35 Owen Chadwick, *The Founding of Cuddesdon* (Oxford: Oxford University Press, 1954), especially chap. 3. For general criticisms of this strategy see M.A. Crowther, *Church Embattled: Religious Controversy in Mid-Victorian England* (Newton Abbot, UK: David and Charles, 1970), 232; and F.W. Bullock, *A History of Training for the Ministry of the Church of England and Wales from 1800 to 1874* (St Leonards-On-Sea: Budd and Gillat, 1955), 95–6. T.A. Reed presents the traditional account in chapter 3 of his history of the college. T.A. Reed, *A History of the University of Trinity College, Toronto 1852–1952* (Toronto: University of Toronto Press, 1952), 60–9. After discussing the force-feeding of students, Cronyn turned to matters of theology, beginning with the undue exaltation of the Virgin Mary. When attacking Trinity College, one of Cronyn's defenders refers to "the woman arrayed in purple and scarlet, who has made all nations drunk with her fornication." See *The Bishop of Huron's Objections to the Theological Teaching of Trinity College, with the Provost's Reply, printed by order of the Corporation of Trinity College* (Toronto: Rowsell and Ellis, 1862); and *Strictures on the Two Letters of Provost Whitaker in Answer to the Charges Brought by the Lord Bishop of Huron Against the Teaching of Trinity College by a Presbyter* (London: Thomas Evans, 1861).

36 "Let Us Have Darkness," *The Grip* 4, no. 18 (27 March 1875).

37 On Wycliffe and the role of the evangelical laity, see Alan Hayes, "The Struggle for the Rights of the Laity in the Diocese of Toronto, 1850–1879," *Journal of the Canadian Church Historical Society* 26 (April 1984): 5–17; *idem*, "Repairing the Walls: Church Reform and Social Reform, 1867–1939," in Alan L. Hayes, ed. *By Grace Coworkers: The Building of the Anglican Diocese of Toronto, 1780–1989* (Toronto: Anglican Book Centre, 1989), 43–95; [Revd J.P. Sheraton], *The History and Principles of Wycliffe College: An Address to the Alumni by the Rev. Principal Sheraton, DD, October*

7th, 1891 (Toronto: J.E. Bryant, 1891); and Revd Professor Dyson Hague, "The History of Wycliffe College," *The Jubilee Volume of Wycliffe College* (Toronto: Wycliffe College, 1927).

38 Trinity College Archives, "A Sermon Preached in the Chapel of Trinity College, Toronto, on Sunday, June 27, 1852, by George Whitaker, MA, published at the request of the students." See also Brian Heeney, *A Different Kind of Gentleman: Parish Clergy as Professional Men in Early Mid-Victorian England* (Hamden, Conn.: Anchor Books, 1976).

39 The literature on this issue is enormous. See Ruby Heap and Allison Prentice, eds, *Gender and Education in Ontario* (Toronto: Scholars Press, 1991); Johanna M. Selles, *Methodists and Women's Education in Ontario, 1836–1925* (Montreal and Kingston: McGill-Queen's University Press, 1996); Marguerite Van Die, ed., *Religion and Public Life in Canada: Historical and Comparative Perspectives* (Toronto: University of Toronto Press, 2001); and Ann Braude, "Women's History *Is* American Religious History," in Thomas A. Tweed, ed., *Retelling US Religious History* (Berkeley: University of California Press, 1997), 87–107.

40 Brian Heeney, *The Women's Movement in the Church of England 1850–1930* (Oxford: Clarendon Press, 1988).

41 Trinity College Archives, Minute Book of Corporation, 9 December 1885.

42 Women were admitted to Trinity College by stages. The first committee of council was struck on 14 February 1883. Women were then allowed to write examinations and receive "certificates," but they were not allowed to keep terms or take degrees. The medical school, however, had decided to admit women, leading the council to give notice of motion on 2 July 1885 that "University statutes be so amended that women may proceed to degrees in Arts and Music as well as in Medicine, as they are now allowed to do so by statute."

The final statute (quoted in the text) was much simpler and more direct. Trinity College Archives, Minute Book of Corporation (for dates indicated). See also Paula J.S. LaPierre, "The First Generation: The Experience of Women University Students in Central Canada" (PhD thesis, Graduate Department of Education, University of Toronto, 1993).

43 Trinity College Archives, Minute Book of Corporation, 14 February 1883. A committee was set up on the motion of William Henderson "to confer with a similar committee of the Bishop Strachan School in regard to affording University facilities to the pupils of that School and also to report to the Council on the whole subject of the higher education of women." See also Kate Rousmaniere, "To Prepare the Ideal Woman: Private Denominational Girls' Schooling in Late-Nineteenth Century Ontario," (MA thesis, Department of Education, University of Toronto, 1984).

44 Trinity College Archives, *The Calendar of the University of Trinity College* (1853), 15.

45 George W. Spragge attributes the resignation of the Faculty of Medicine in 1856 to the continuing demand for religious tests. The faculty had tried to get around these provisions by admitting "occasional students" who would complete their courses at Trinity and then apply for their degrees elsewhere. The council (and especially Whitaker) refused to sanction this practice, and the faculty resigned. When the Faculty of Medicine was reinstated in 1871, however, a compromise of sorts was reached: provision was made for students to petition to dispense with this test on religious grounds. George W. Spragge, "Trinity Medical College," *Ontario History* 58 (June 1966): 63–98.

46 A.H. Crowfoot, *Benjamin Cronyn: First Bishop of Huron* (London: Diocese of Huron, 1957); and *This Dreamer: Life of Issac Hellmuth: Second Bishop of Huron* (Toronto: Copp Clark, 1963).

47 D.C. Masters, "The Anglican Evangelicals in Toronto, 1870–1900," *Journal of the Canadian Church Historical Society* 20 (1978); Alan Hayes, "The Making of an Evangelical Cathedral, 1839–1883," in William Cooke, ed., *The Parish and Cathedral of St James, Toronto, 1797–1997* (Toronto: University of Toronto Press, 1998), 39–76. William H. Katerburg, *Modernity and the Dilemma of North American Anglican Identities, 1800–1950* (Montreal and Kingston: McGill-Queen's University Press, 2001). See also material on Wycliffe College cited above.

48 The college accounts, nonetheless, still included the unpaid subscriptions in the endowment, where they inflated the health of the endowment but did not earn any income. Subscriptions were payable in instalments. The financial records make it clear that the college had great difficulty collecting even the initial payment. Trinity College Archives, Minute Book of Corporation, 30 March 1852.

49 Trinity College Archives, Land Book, vol. 1. Lot no. 12 was sold to Adam Elliot in February 1865 for £800. Whitney described the college's holdings in the rear half of lot no. 12 in the seventh concession of Augusta Township in the following terms: "This is a swamp lot. The timber consists of Cedar, Hemlock, with a little pine, elm, and ash. In the spring of the year I am informed the lot is from six to ten inches under water." The Land Book is one of the beautiful holdings in the college archives.

50 Ontario Archives, Strachan Papers, Memorandum Concerning Trinity College, 1862.

51 Trinity College Archives, Minute Book of Corporation, 8 March 1856.

52 SPG Archives, D Series, Toronto 1860–1867, Strachan to Hawkins, 30 March 1860.

53 William Gooderham had taken an active part on the original board and had contributed £10 to Trinity College for each of his twelve children.

54 SPG Archives, C Series, C/Canada/Toronto, Folio 518 (John Strachan), Strachan to SPG, 15 March 1852.

55 Perhaps the strongest testimony to the weakness of the college's financial position was the fact that within ten years of the campaign that had opened with such promise, the Bishop of Toronto had to appeal to the government for support. In 1861 he wrote to the Attorney General for Canada West, the Hon. John A. Macdonald, endorsing a memorial from the Synod of the Diocese of Toronto for "pecuniary aid to Trinity College." It seems ironic, given the recent events, that Strachan closed his letter with the words "I trust the gift will be generous and free from conditions." Ontario Archives, Strachan Letter Book, Letter to the Honble John A McDonald [sic], Attorney General West, 16 Nov 1861. Alan Hayes discusses the problems with Cameron's failures. See Alan L. Hayes, "Repairing the Walls: Church Reform and Social Reform, 1867–1939," in Alan L. Hayes, ed., *By Grace Co-workers: The Building of the Anglican Diocese of Toronto, 1780–1989* (Toronto: Anglican Book Centre, 1989), 43–95; and Donanld Swainson, "John Hillyard Cameron," in *Dictionary of Canadian Biography*, vol. 10 (Toronto: University of Toronto Press, 1972), 118–23.

56 Ontario Archives, Strachan Papers, P.B. De Blaquiere to Bishop of Toronto, 19 May 1851.

57 Elwood H. Jones, *St John's Peterborough: The Sesquicentennial History of an Anglican Parish, 1826–1976* (Peterborough: Maxwell Review, 1976).

58 Journal of the Synod of the Church of England in the Diocese of Toronto, App. R (1) (Toronto: Rowsell and Hutchison, 1872).

59 Trinity's response to these charges was very weak. For example, it claimed that the number of graduates was 151 (raising the average per year from six to eight). It then went on to point out that seventy-eight students "[had] left without proceeding to a degree" and of these fifteen "[had] been admitted to Holy Orders." Both of these

admissions were in themselves devastating criticisms of the college. Trinity College Archives, Minute Book of Corporation, 15 January 1873.

60 Ontario Archives, Strachan Papers, Strachan to Metcalfe, 6 March 1844.

61 The rivalry between these two "systems" of education was understood clearly by both sides. For his part, Strachan wanted Trinity to have its own "Eton" (and an alliance with church grammar schools). Peter Boyle De Blaquiere, the Chancellor of the University of Toronto, opposed a royal charter for Trinity because the new college was "calculated to undermine our National education as now in successful operation both in the Common and Grammar Schools and the National University." It should also be pointed out that Whitaker refused the offer of a seat on the Senate of the University of Toronto on the grounds that, because the two institutions were "distinct and independent societies, and founded on widely different principles, it is not expedient that any officer of the one should accept an appointment in the other." See "Pastoral Letter to the Clergy and Laity of the Diocese of Toronto," as quoted in Henry Melville, MD, in *The Rise and Progress of Trinity College, Toronto; with a Sketch of the Life of the Lord Bishop of Toronto as Connected with Church Education in Canada* (Toronto: Henry Rowsell, 1852), 93; Ontario Archives, Strachan Papers, P.B. De Blaquiere to Bishop of Toronto, 19 May 1851; Trinity College Archives, Minute Book of Corporation, 4 March 1854.

EPILOGUE

1 This is the title given to Bishop Strachan in the dedication to the official history of Trinity College. "*Ad Piam Memoriam Johannis Strachan Fundatoris Nostri.*" See T.A. Reed, *A History of the University of Trinity College, Toronto, 1852–1952* (Toronto: University of Toronto Press, 1952), v.

2 When Strachan died and left his library to the College a fund was established "for the erection of a Library and Convocation Hall at Trinity College, as a Memorial to the Founder." The largest donation was $100, and the appeals for contributions were apparently discontinued after one year. Trinity College Archives, *The Calendar of the University of Trinity College for the Year 1868, Calendar of the University of Trinity College* (1869).

3 The new convocation hall was funded by a special gift of the Henderson family; it was officially opened with the installation of the new chancellor, George William Allan, on 15 November 1877. Trinity College Archives, *Calendar of the University of Trinity College* (1878).

4 A lodge was built to the north of the college to house the Provost's large family, although the date and builder are not clear. On 7 October 1862 the council received a bill for the balance owing "for work done at the College and the Provost's house" from "Thos. Storm, Arch." Trinity College Archives, Minute Book of Corporation, 7 October 1862.

5 On 10 May 1871, the council changed the statutes to allow students to petition the chancellor or vice chancellor to dispense with the declaration that they were "truly and sincerely" members of the United Church of England and Ireland on the grounds that they were not members of the church. At the same time the corporation was given the power, if it saw "good cause," to allow "any Professor or Professors of the Faculty of Medicine, to dispense with the above mentioned qualification and subscriptions." As George W. Spragge points out, opposition to these tests seems to have come mainly from the Faculty of Medicine, which left the college over this issue and only returned when this dispensation was approved. Not only did the faculty want to increase enrolments, but it also wanted to draw upon the teaching expertise of non-Anglican doctors.

In affirming the Anglican character of the college, the corporation was quick to point out, rather ungenerously, that no changes would be made in "the religious teaching of the College" to accommodate "the opinions of those who are not members of the Church of England." Trinity College Archives, Minute Book of Corporation, 10 May 1871.

6 SPG Archives, D Series, D Toronto 1860–7, 710.

7 The Minute Book of Corporation makes several references to student opposition to various aspects of college discipline. These took the form of petitions to change the rules to occasions when the corporation had to note the punishment meted out for students who had broken the rules. See, for example, "Memorial from undergraduates concerning aspects of College discipline" presented by the students on 10 February 1863. This was rejected by the members of corporation, who told the students to "give such attention to their studies as will meet the approval of the Professors." The petition concerning the wearing of the cap and gown came before council on 11 December 1866 and it was agreed that the cap (but not the gown) could be dispensed with "in the streets" during winter. On 9 November 1869 students were allowed to dispense with the cap and gown outside the College between 2:00 and 6:00 p.m. Trinity College Archives, Minute Book of Corporation, 10 February 1863, 11 December 1866, 9 November 1869. Strachan's own grandson was confined "to gates" for not attending chapel. Ontario Archives, Strachan Letter Book, Copy of Letter from Professor Edward Kendall, 18 July 1860.

8 The college curriculum is described in chapter 2. The new courses that were introduced served a variety of purposes. Dr Bovell's lectures became an important part of the curriculum (and were required for that reason); Professor Hind's lectures in chemistry and geology were treated as a part of mathematics, which always included some "science"; there were also "new" and popular subjects such as modern languages and drawing and fine art. Surveying and fortifi-

cation, which were offered until 1868, may have been a response to the unsettled state of the Niagara frontier at this time.

9 "Preached in Trinity College Chapel on Sunday June 20, 1880, Being the last Sunday in the Academical Year," *Sermons Preached in Toronto for the Most Part in the Chapel of Trinity College by George Whitaker, MA* (London: Rivingtons; Toronto: Willing and Williamson, 1882), 306–23.

10 For a discussion of this election and Sweatman's fascinating career, see Alan L. Hayes, "Repairing the Walls: Church Reform and Social Reform, 1867–1939," in Alan L. Hayes, ed., *By Grace Co- workers: The Building of the Anglican Diocese of Toronto, 1780–1989* (Toronto: Anglican Book Centre, 1989), 43–95. For more material on Sweatman, see Diocese of Toronto Archives, Obituary Files, "A Scrapbook on the Death of Bishop Sweatman, 1909."

11 Trinity College Archives, Minute Book of Corporation, 27 June 1879. The council passed a resolution offering Whitaker's son the professorship of theology and "the right of succession to the office of Provost on its vacancy." See also Christopher Fergus Headon, "George Whitaker," *Dictionary of Canadian Biography*, vol. 11 (Toronto: University of Toronto Press, 1982), 916–17; and C.T. McIntire, "The Making of Christian Gentlemen: The Social Message of Provost George Whitaker in Trinity College, Toronto, 1851–81" (unpublished article).

12 Trinity College Archives, Minute Book of Corporation, 23 September 1879, 29 January 1880, 17 February 1880, 12 May 1880, 3 June 1880, 7 April 1881, 13 July 1881.

13 See especially A.C.L. Haig, "The Church, the Universities and Learning in Late Victorian England," *The Historical Journal* 29, no. 1 (1986); 187–201.

14 Trinity College Archives, Minute Book of Corporation, 12 October 1881.

15 Ibid.

16 Ibid., 12 July 1882.

17 Ibid.

18 Ibid.; *Calendar of the University of Trinity College* (1882) (1883). In 1882 the old religious test was waived for non-Anglicans; in 1883 it was done away with completely and replaced by the declaration of allegiance to the Queen. See also Minute Book of Corporation, 12 July 1882.

19 Trinity College Archives, *Calendar of the University of Trinity College* (1879).

20 Ibid., *Calendar of the University of Trinity College* (1882), 48.

21 Trinity College Archives, Minute Book of Corporation, 13 July 1881. What became of Mrs Morrison is not clear. When this position was raised to the rank of lecturer in the academic year 1882–3 the college hired a man, the Revd H.W. Parker of the Philadelphia School of Oratory. Langtry at that time held "the lectureship in Apologetics." On 23 May 1883 he resigned from the curriculum committee, and on 20 June 1883 he resigned his lectureship. He then took up parochial work but returned to corporation as a member elected by the graduates. He later became the leading figure in the opposition to federation with the University of Toronto.

22 Ibid., 13 September 1882, 14 February 1883, 20 June 1883, 2 July 1885, 9 December 1885.

23 Paula J.S. LaPierre, "The First Generation: The Experience of Women University Students in Central Canada" (PhD thesis, Graduate Department of Education, University of Toronto, 1993). Body himself, while supporting the admission of women, opposed the coeducation of women, and with the establishment of St Hilda's College in 1888, instituted a system of separate lectures for men and women, which was then abandoned in 1894 for financial reasons. For a contemporary account of some of the hostility women faced (and their ability to deal with it), see Ethel Middleton, "Life at St

Hilda's," 88–90, *St Hilda's Chronicle*, vol. 3, no. 2, (Trinity term, 1903), 39–40; see also Elsie Gregory MacGill, *My Mother the Judge: A Biography of Helen Gregory MacGill* (Toronto: Ryerson Press, 1955).

24 Trinity College Archives, Minute Book of Corporation, 10 March 1886 (Convocation), 15 December 1886 (broaden appeal within the church).

25 Trinity College Archives, Minute Book of Corporation, 1 March 1894.

26 "Trinity College," *The Mitre*, volume VI, number 4, February 1899.

27 T.A. Reed, *A History of the University of Trinity College, Toronto, 1852–1952* (Toronto: University of Toronto Press, 1952), 266.

28 Trinity College Archives, Minute Book of Corporation, 15 May 1889.

29 Ibid.,"Report of Proposed Scheme of University Confederation," 16 January 1885; "Report of the Subcommittee upon the Subject of University Federation," 14 March 1900.

Illustration Credits

"St George's Church, Toronto from My dressing room Window July
1851" by A.R. Crease. Toronto Reference Library, J. Ross Robertson
Collection (MTL 1158)

Elms in Ravine: *Trinity College, Toronto* (Menzies, Toronto, 1914),
photo 14b

Bishop Strachan: Trinity College Archives (P1098/1001)

Matriculation register: Trinity College Archives, Matriculation Register
(990-0053/039)

King's College: University of Toronto Archives (B1993-0051)

Robert Baldwin: Toronto Reference Library (MTL 1865)

East wing, University College: University of Toronto Archives (A1965-
0004 [1.8])

University College, southeast: University of Toronto Archives
(B1965–1071)

Revd John McCaul: University of Toronto Archives (A1965-0019/004)

Revd James Beaven: *University of Toronto Monthly* 3, no. 8 (December
1902), facing page 69

Receipt: Trinity College Archives (986-0098/004)

Banner: Trinity College Archives (P1098/1102)

Constitution: Trinity College Archives, Minute Book of Corporation
(986-0001/012)

Revd Alexander Bethune: Trinity College Archives (P1098/1186)

Diocesan Theological Institute: *Trinity College, Toronto* (Menzies,
Toronto, 1914), photo 27a

St Aidan's College: *The Builder* (6 April 1850), 162

Trinity College: Henry Melville, *The Rise and Progress of Trinity
College, Toronto*

Minutes: *A Charge Delivered to the Clergy of the Diocese of Toronto in
May MDCCCLI by John, Lord Bishop of Toronto* (Toronto: Diocesan
Press, 1851)

Trinity College: *Trinity College, Toronto* (Toronto: Menzies, 1914),
photo 27b

Plan: Henry Melville, *The Rise and Progress of Trinity College, Toronto*.
Provost Whitaker has added to his copy of Melville's history, now in
the Trinity College archives, a sketch of the Convocation Hall, added
to the building in 1877.

Chapel: *Trinity College, Toronto* (Toronto: Menzies, 1914), photo 10b

Entrance gates: *Trinity College, Toronto* (Toronto: Menzies, 1914),
photo 13

Letter: Trinity College Archives, Minute Book of Corporation
(986-0001/012)

George Whitaker: Trinity College Archives (P1098/1002)

Revd E. Parry: *Trinity College, Toronto* (Toronto: Menzies, 1914),
photo 18d

Revd George Irving: Trinity College Archives (P1043)

Calendar: Trinity College Archives (990-0053/014)

Challenge: *Trinity College Conducted as a Mere Boys' School, Not as a
College* (Toronto, 1858), Trinity College Archives

Questions: *Strictures on the Two Letters of Provost Whitaker in Answer
to Charges Brought by the Lord Bishop of Huron against the Teaching
of Trinity College* (London, C.W. Thomas Evans, 1861)

St Hilda's College: *Trinity College, Toronto* (Toronto: Menzies, 1914),
photo 9

C.W.E. Body: Trinity College Archives (P1098/1009)

Index

Numbers in italics refer to illustrations, which follow the page number given.